GOOD INTENTIONS

Also in the CrossCurrents Series

GOOD INTENTIONS

*Writing Center Work
for Postmodern Times*

NANCY MALONEY GRIMM

AFTERWORD BY NANCY G. BARRON

CrossCurrents
New Perspectives in Rhetoric and Composition
CHARLES I. SCHUSTER, SERIES EDITOR

Boynton/Cook Publishers
HEINEMANN
PORTSMOUTH, NH

For students
past, present, future

Boynton/Cook Publishers, Inc.
A subsidiary of Reed Elsevier Inc.
361 Hanover Street
Portsmouth, NH 03801–3912
http://www.boyntoncook.com

Offices and agents throughout the world

The author and publisher wish to thank those who have generously given permission to reprint borrowed material:

Excerpts from "'Whispers of Coming and Going': Lessons from Fannie" by Anne DiPardo. From *The Writing Center Journal* (Volume 12, No. 2, 1992). Reprinted by permission of the Publisher.

Portions of Chapter Four, "Getting Unstuck: Rearticulating the Nodal Points," by Nancy Maloney Grimm originally appeared as "Rearticulating the Work of the Writing Center" by Nancy Maloney Grimm. *College Composition and Communication* (Volume 47, No. 4, 1996). Reprinted by permission of the Publisher.

Library of Congress Cataloging-in-Publication Data

Grimm, Nancy Maloney.
    Good intentions : writing center work for postmodern times /
Nancy Maloney Grimm.
      p. cm.—(CrossCurrents)
    Includes index.
    ISBN 0-86709-487-7
    1. English language—Rhetoric—Study and teaching. 2. Report writing—
Study and teaching. 3. Pluralism (Social sciences) 4. Writing centers. 5. Post-
modernism. I. Title. II. Series: Crosscurrents (Portsmouth, NH)
PE1404.G695   1999
808'.042'07—dc21   99–14465
                                     CIP

Editor: Lisa Luedeke
Production: Elizabeth Valway
Cover design: Jenny Jensen Greenleaf
Manufacturing: Louise Richardson

Printed in the United States of America on acid-free paper
Docutech T & C 2004

Contents

"The road to hell is paved with good intentions."

—Edward J. Maloney

Acknowledgments

The final pages of this book list the many scholars whose work has made mine possible. In addition to these people, most of whom I know only through their published work, many others have supported me in important ways. I cannot possibly name all the teachers, relatives, friends, and colleagues who have offered encouragement and inspiration over the years, but I would like to thank a special few.

I am thankful for all the people whose comments about literacy and the writing center have made me angry. My inability to provide quick counterarguments fueled the research that led to this book. I am also grateful for the many students who have worked with me in the writing center. By sharing honestly and generously of themselves, they created the commitment that kept me writing at the computer.

Thanks to family members whose love supported my work, particularly Tom Grimm, Kristin Grimm, Ben Grimm, Rita Ori, Monica Kane, the camp gang, Richard Maloney, Nancy Burke, Edmund Burke, and Bridie Conroy Grimm.

Many colleagues in the Humanities Department at Michigan Technological University have provided friendship, encouragement, and insightful revision comments. Marilyn Cooper, Cindy Selfe, and Diana George deserve special mention, as does Max Seel, dean of the College of Sciences and Arts, all of whom suffered through the earliest draft of this book as members of my dissertation committee.

I am especially grateful to three women, whom I am blessed to have as both good friends and good colleagues. Sylvia Matthews, Pam Wehr, and Jean Blanning have shared generously of their time, compassion, and practical wisdom for many years. Every writer should have a reader like Sylvia, who from the beginning believed passionately in this project. In addition, my spirit guides, Debbie Dlubala, Rosie LeVeque, Sheila Marks, and Ann Wilmers, have helped me balance my life, which makes my work possible.

As editor of the CrossCurrents Series, Chuck Schuster has refined the art of Max Perkins through his ability to push for revision with humor, perception, and appropriate detachment. My efforts greatly benefited from his seasoned good advice. I am grateful also for the careful work of the talented production, design, and editing staff at Heinemann.

During the last two years, my most faithful and challenging reader and friend has been Nancy Barron. Without her intelligent, good-natured critiques, I would have written a much duller and more confusing book. Without her stories about school experience so different from my own, I would have lost my motivation. Without her friendship, I would have missed the laughter and warmth that feed the soul.

Finally, I thank my parents, who, although long deceased, imbued their children with a work ethic, a passion for social justice, and a love for learning that has lasted all these years.

None of the above should be held responsible for any faults in this final version, which are entirely my own.

Introduction

For two weeks every summer, my two sisters and their families join my family at our camp on the shores of Lake Superior. While our children occupy themselves making desserts, playing cards, pumping up leaky inner tubes, and resurrecting old games, my sisters and I often sit together and work on sewing projects while we tell stories about our lives and exchange mutual concerns. One summer, the three of us gathered on the porch in green-and-white-striped deck chairs. Monica and I were beginning new quilting projects, and Cis offered to read to us from her new quilting book while we sewed. She read stories about modern sewers whose new markers contained chemicals that eventually rotted their finished quilts, about overly eager sewers who skipped their basting and ended up with badly bunched-up backings, and about hurried sewers who didn't prewash fabrics and were later dismayed over shrunken, shapeless quilts. The stories provoked worries, haunted our hastily made decisions about our two-week projects, and threatened our pleasure in sewing together.

What these stories didn't take into account were our *reasons* for starting our projects, reasons connected with friends and family. Monica was developing a friendship with the woman who had shared the quilt design with her. I was anticipating my son's graduation from college, making him an Amish wall quilt like the one he liked in our family room. Neither of us had started these projects with perfect products in mind, but instead as our traditional way of passing time together—calming our busy-ness, sharing friendship, offering a gift from the heart. The quilting stories in Cis' new book distracted us from our original intentions, from our involvement in the moment, and turned the projects' pleasures into worries. In the long run, we learned from this discomfort, paid more attention to the details of our next project, and even looked for other stories that helped resolve our quilting troubles.

Theory often works in much the same way as the quilting stories, haunting and worrying us and only sometimes instructing us in practical decisions. Because theory is powerful, it often overtakes practice, alienates us from our intentions, silences what we know about what we do, and subjugates the daily knowledge that might challenge it. Sometimes—and far less commonly—theory arises out of failed practice, when pressing problems challenge us to find new organizing principles and to make sense of what happened. But new theories arise out of failed practice only when we can silence old commonsense theories long enough to acknowledge tensions and to complicate our thinking. At times like this, revised theories offer backward lessons, providing foresight through hindsight, allowing today's contradictions to shape tomorrow's practice.

This book considers the conflicting function of writing centers, and my goal is to make well-intentioned people uncomfortable. I write to disrupt the good intentions not only of the people who don't understand the value of writing centers but also, most important, of the people who think they do. My hope is that uncomfortable people will search for more complicated understandings of what writing center work entails. I hope this book will be read not only by writing center directors but also by the undergraduate and graduate students who work in writing centers, by composition teachers whose students use writing centers, and by theorists and practitioners who imagine a social future in which literacy practices enable us to communicate across differences.

My writing center history began in 1978 when I was hired as a tutor making an hourly wage. Although I now direct the writing center from a tenure-track faculty position, my work history includes many years in part-time, temporary full-time, and professional staff positions. In 1990, I began working toward a Ph.D. while I continued to direct both the writing center and the other learning centers on our campus. As I read theory in graduate seminars, I searched for ways to understand literacy learning, to articulate what I learn from writing center practice, and to explain the work of the writing center to the university. This book results from that period of intense searching and reading. Theorizing became a habitual search for the conceptual language that helps me articulate the understandings arising from working in a contact zone. Like the quilting stories, theorizing has disrupted the good intentions that informed earlier decision making and challenged me to revise practices. But theorizing also helps me break through frustration and inarticulateness and turn the chip on my shoulder into an instrument of analysis. I liken this approach to other necessary labor-intensive undertakings with delayed and sometimes unpredictable results.

Gardening. Lugging around bags of peat and manure in humid weather, digging and pitching rocks, swatting at black flies and mosquitoes, weeding swamp grass again and again, gardening in the Upper Peninsula of Michigan can be uncomfortable work. My "yard" is a thin layer of dirt thrown over mine rock, and to grow lilacs or roses, I need to enrich the soil with bags of manure. The analogy is not accidental. Although practitioners resist theory, sometimes calling it "a bunch of

BS," it is theory that makes the terrain fertile, capable of sustaining growth. The dirty, back-bruising work pays off later in the season or in future summers when roots take hold, trees spread shade, and flowers please the eyes. I use theory like I use fertilizer, to grow ideas and to enrich the context for decision making.

Mapmaking. Theorizing, like mapmaking, is an activity that offers a heightened sense of position, a keener awareness of where the writing center is in relationship to other social systems and ideas. The act of theorizing necessarily maps out territory, just as the act of gardening names a portion of the yard as garden. Mapmaking can be an act of colonizing, of making a space suit specifications and preferences. In writing about this power of maps, Denis Wood warns that unless we continuously question the map, "the map will disable us from acting with intelligence and grace, will doom us to a living that is fatally flawed, partial, and incomplete" (1992, 26). With Stuart Hall, I believe that theorizing in a postmodern context creates a pressing need to go on theorizing, rejecting "the finality of a finished theoretical paradigm"(1986, 60).

Fixing things. From James Raymond I borrow the image of the *bricoleur* or "fix-it man" as another metaphor for theorizing. The theoretical bricoleur finds theory "always unsatisfactory and often useful," a "tool that sometimes works rather than a model of the way things are." Theories are perspectives that "yield useful insights in this situation or that, but always partial insights, never the whole truth" (1989, 389). The fix-it man understands that the fix is only temporary, that he will be called upon again because his understanding of how things work is always partial. Theoretical bricolage "resists the desire for panaceas" and "exploits home remedies." It is always on the watch for blind spots, always examining assumptions, always recognizing limits. For the theoretical bricoleur, progress is the discovery of blind spots that leads to amending theory.

Quilt making. To the masculine image of the bricoleur I add the feminine image of the quilt maker who traditionally works from necessity and with fragments, the bits and pieces of what is at hand, sometimes mixing the already used fabric of an old dress or suit with the remnants of a newly cut piece. [B]ell hooks describes her grandmother using quilting as a "space to calm down and come back to herself" (1990, 117). I write this book from scraps of time rescued during a day at work, from pieces cut from vacation days, from used conference papers, from theory found in the books littering my porch and my study, from ideas offered by friends and colleagues. And just as hooks' grandmother found quilting a "meditative practice . . . pleasing to the mind and heart," a work of material and aesthetic necessity, I put together this theorizing to order my own thinking, to find meaning in my daily work in the writing center, to ease both intellectual and emotional frustration. Like the practical quilt maker, I hope that the results of my theorizing will be put to everyday use.

Cultivating, mapmaking, fixing, and quilt making are efforts to make things grow, to change fixed conceptions, to put together what has been apart in order to make things work, and to join bits of available materials and put the result to everyday use. For me, theorizing writing center practice is an effort to get at meaning in daily events, to gain a heightened sense of where writing centers are in the social and institutional structure, and to change the professional context that questions the value of this work. Theorizing is an effort to uncover the assumptions that guide a practice and to imagine alternatives. I interrupt theorizing with storytelling, hoping to limit closure, render the theory incomplete, and leave the terrain open for additional exploration, mapping, and linkages.

The nexus of two centuries is an important time for retheorizing the work of a writing center, particularly the way that writing centers interact with the differences of race, class, culture, and education. As technologies shrink our national borders and as our population changes, the United States is more challenged than ever to figure out what it means to be a multicultural democracy. Although we Americans pride ourselves on our diversity, we have yet to figure out how to live with differences. Too often writing centers are expected to "manage" those differences, to bring them under control, to make students with difference sound as mainstream as possible. Under this expectation, writing center directors too easily become administrators rather than theorists. We might, for example, worry too much about how to "deal with" nonnative speakers of English who come to the writing center rather than think about why they come and what qualifies us to work with them. What do monolingual language users know about the tacit ways that language functions to indicate time, order, structure, shades of meaning, qualification, and ownership? Regional dialects, ethnic, racial, and class variations, and the accents of immigrant populations still provoke emotional responses. We are a nation formed by immigrant populations, yet we also colonized native peoples. We celebrate (and market) ethnicity in summer festivals, yet we enact English-only laws. The American belief in democracy hinges on the belief that literacy education can resolve inequities, but there are fault lines within that belief. While literacy is supposed to guarantee access to education and jobs, at the same time it works as a gatekeeper, preventing access and demanding submission to a standard in exchange for passage.

In higher education, many of the unresolved anxieties about literacy come to rest in writing centers. Students from working-class backgrounds, from minority cultures, and from other nations arrive at writing centers feeling that their efforts to write in the mainstream culture are not understood. Students who have learning disabilities, students who are confused about assignment expectations, and students who are trying to write in an unfamiliar discourse or genre also find their way to writing centers. Writing center workers are often conflicted about how much "help" to provide these students, about their relationship to faculty, about their role in the university. Questions are repeatedly raised about the ethics of writing center work: how much help is too much? Are students capable of "doing their own work?" How much time is legitimate to spend with each student? Although universities establish writing centers to demonstrate their commitment to literacy, the value of the writing center is often questioned at funding time and the position of the writing center director in the institutional hierarchy is often subject to debate. Some faculty would like the writing center director to find the perfect computer software to help students write clear paragraphs.

Even within the field of composition studies, writing centers are often overlooked. At the 1993 "Composition in the 21st Century" conference, sponsored by the Council of Writing Program Administrators, speakers identified challenges that we face in higher education in the next century. Most of the issues identified—the need for more complicated understandings of authorship, of identity construction, of multiculturalism, of home literacies, of literacy standards—are grappled with every day in a writing center, but not one speaker acknowledged (except when pressed to do so by members of the audience) that writing centers are already crucibles for these issues.

Writing centers cannot resolve the national confusion about literacy, but I believe that over time they can contribute to a deeper understanding of literacy and to more democratic approaches to literacy education. To do this, writing centers need to be more fully engaged with the paradox of literacy—the way that literacy both dominates and liberates, both demands submission and offers the promise of agency. I believe that the cultural changes we call postmodernity offer writing centers opportunities for this engagement. In this book, I use theory to challenge commonsense understandings and to move writing centers into productive engagement with the conflicts in literacy education.

In 1984, Stephen North observed that writing centers are thought of as "a kind of obscure backwater" and "no place for a scholar" (1984a, 444). To challenge the notion of a writing center as an obscure backwater—a stagnant or backward place—I play on the the term *backwater* by *back watering* (reversing motion by the placement of an oar) the writing center into theoretical waters. Theorizing is often dismissed as something that might be useful for ontological discussions but not for practical decision making. As an example of the effect of theorizing on daily lives, look at the feminist consciousness raising that occurred in the late sixties and early seventies. Theorizing about gender and identity transformed the lives of many Anglo women because theory challenged naturalized assumptions, offered ways of naming conflicts, encouraged women to share stories, and offered visions of a world in which the social processes of gendering could be resisted. Theorizing gave us the courage to go back to school, to revise our role in the family, to insist on shared responsibility for household chores, and to challenge taken-for-granted workplace practices. Theorizing offered women reasons to believe that the pervasive limited images of women found everywhere—in elementary school textbooks, in media representations, in magazine advertising—could and should be resisted.

Theorizing itself does not solve daily writing center problems, but because it multiplies the perspectives we bring to problems, it can change practices. In the Michigan Technological University Writing Center, for example, theorizing heightened our awareness of the subtle remains of remedial language. To emphasize our focus on developing talent and strategy and on identifying multiple options for writing positions and rhetorical moves, we decided to call ourselves *writing coaches* rather than *tutors*. This change suggested new metaphors for promoting the writing center at points of entrance to the university, particularly at orientation sessions for new students and new faculty. As the writing center became linked to recruitment efforts and proactive academic success, it became less vulnerable to budget cuts. As we explored theories of literacy that emphasized the social importance of literacy relationships, we decided to track students who had weekly writing center appointments and discovered that they also had higher-than-average persistence rates. The favorable impact of the writing center on retention rates led to the development of learning centers in math and chemistry, then in physics and biology, then in engineering. The conceptual energies of theorizing affect not just the way we think about our practices but the way we talk about them, the way others perceive them, the way we enact them, and the effects they have on others.

Resistance to theorizing in writing center circles comes from a concern for theory's universalizing tendencies. More than ten years ago, Stephen North observed that the "helter-skelter" growth of writing centers created such diversity in programs that "theory- or pedagogy-based research questions simply cannot meet universal political approval" (1984b, 28). North noted that the diversity in writing center programs made it difficult to explain what any writing center does beyond saying that a writing center offers some kind of support for writing. That diversity in programming persists. On some campuses, writing centers are chiefly computer writing environments; others support faculty who are developing a writing-across-the-curriculum program; others work with students in specific curriculums such as business or law. Some writing centers are staffed by professional writing consultants, and others employ undergraduates. Some serve as drop-in centers whereas others offer courses for credit or semester-long weekly appointments. I believe that diversity in programming and responsiveness to local contexts are essential to the vitality of writing centers. Rather than dismiss the wisdom of carefully considering local conditions, I argue that writing center workers also need theoretical understandings.

In this book I bring theoretical understandings into contact with daily writing center practice in order to extend decisions about practice beyond consideration of the local context. I theorize in order to ask questions about what's missing or what is misrepresented, to hear the silent responses. For me, one of the satisfactions of writing center work is figuring out the tacit expectations of academic literacy and making those expectations explicit for the students who want to "make it." My maternal grandmother and her sisters, who immigrated from Ireland to the United States in their late teens, were involved in a similar project. They found jobs working as maids for wealthy families and used their savings to bring over additional members of the family. Through careful observation in the homes of their employers, they learned how the rich people dressed for dinner, how to set the dinner table with a tablecloth and properly placed silverware, how to put the ketchup and mayonnaise in serving dishes, how to converse with strangers outside one's social class. They took these lessons home, applying them to the newly arrived family members and later to their children and grandchildren. With raised chins and no trace of a smile, they responded to the "but-why" whines of children with the refrain "Because that's the way the rich people does it."

Their work ethic, combined with attention to the details of what mattered to the rich and powerful, contributed to the success of later generations. Yet this success in assimilating and acculturating had its costs. In the process of accommodating to the demands of others, they separated work from personal pleasure. Preparing the house and setting the table for a holiday dinner under my mother's watchful eyes was more a military drill than an art or an exercise in family togetherness. In the hurry to assimilate, they left behind the stories of a childhood in another country and the ability to name things and people in another language. The ethnic groups who came later and threatened the family's hard-earned success were dismissed as backward, and we children were told to avoid interaction with them.

As a member of the generation that profited from the previous generations' work, I was able to raise my children in middle-class circumstances. I am aware of the debt I owe to the labor of the previous generations, but I am also aware of the losses. My paternal grand-mother, an immigrant from Lithuania, disguised her heritage, changed the family name and suppressed her native language. When in the late 1950s, I learned the family's secret (and shameful?) heritage from my older cousins, I could not find Lithuania on a map because it had been absorbed by the Soviet Union. Part of my history had been erased on both a political and personal level. Because so much unresolved family tension was associated with the secret, I was forbidden to discuss it.

In a similar fashion, because writing centers are places where as-similation into the discursive systems of the university is facilitated, one rarely hears stories about the erasures: the loss of motivation, the com-promise of creativity, the silencing of family stories, the impediments to agency, the suppression of other literacies and worldviews. When we learn the discourses we need in order to be accepted in certain groups, we don't always know what to do with the language and knowledge we leave behind. My maternal and paternal grandparents came from countries where they were forbidden to speak their native languages, where the culture of the conqueror, oppressor, colonizer attempted to override their own. Both sides of the family took tremendous risks, made tremendous sacrifices in order for the next generation to live and speak freely. That history is more in my blood and dreams than in my memory because it was forced below language, yet it is that history that troubles me when I see representations of writing center work as inno-cent and ideologically neutral.

In my theorizing, I hold to a vision of literacy education in which accommodation is mutual and personally transformative, in which his-tory does not have to be erased and systems become more flexible. I be-lieve that writing centers can transcend the gatekeeping function of lit-eracy work. Instead of representing writing centers as adjunct sites of service, I theorize them as sites of participatory research into students' literacy practices and as sites of knowledge about the ways that dis-course regulates who we are and who we can be. I invite the under-graduates who work in writing centers to join in the intellectual work of understanding the ways that literacy regulates our relationships with institutions and with one another, and I ask them to imagine ways we can intervene in that regulation.

In this book, I theorize writing center practice to foreground its po-tential for more public and political action. I don't attempt to limit the important work of showing students how literacy functions in higher education, but I do try to move writing centers beyond individualized instruction and into public projects with participatory roles for writing center students. In a groundbreaking 1998 essay about service learn-ing, Aaron Schutz and Anne Ruggles Gere delicately undermine the ethic of care upon which many tutoring programs are based. They argue that an ethic of care is limited to the extent that it depends on a dichotomy between public and private, individual and social. As long as writing center workers view themselves as having the expertise the student needs in order to manage academically, their ability to see beyond a needy individual to a less-than-perfect social structure is blocked. As the work of Schutz and Gere and Bruce Herzberg (1994) indicates, when tutoring is based on a private ethic of care it cannot dislodge individualistic and meritocratic views of school success.

By insisting that writing center workers need to theorize their practice in terms of political and ideological issues, I don't mean to suggest that theorizing will somehow save a fledgling writing center. The practical moves and the considered response to local conditions that help achieve funding and stability are still essential to writing center efforts. However, once a writing center achieves stability, the greater challenge is to ask if the writing center constructs a space for acknowledging the arbitrariness of academic practices and the possibility that these practices unintentionally oppress some students. Postmodernity has made us aware of the inadequacies of universalizing logic and perspective. Because it undermines belief in good intentions and academic practices based on modernist principles, it confronts us with the need to ask how writing centers maintain the status quo, thereby oppressing the very students most dependent on writing center assistance.

I don't believe that any particular theory provides answers to the daily concerns that arise out of writing center practice nor do I believe that theory has direct application to practice. Rather, I believe that in order to work toward more socially just practices of literacy education, we need to rethink the present system that uses literacy to mark differences and make exclusions, and theorizing can help us do that. As they presently operate, writing centers are more often normalizing agents, performing the institutional function of erasing differences. There are very powerful forces working against the opportunities to engage differently. For most writing center workers, particularly those who were successful mainstream students, the strength to resist what feels natural, the desire to question the system that positions them favorably, and the ability to see what before was invisible has to come from the kind of intellectual engagement that can critique the status quo, and it has to take that engagement into the side-by-side work they do with students in the writing center.

In each of the following chapters, I nibble at the whole of writing center work as I know it, applying a notion of institutional change called the Swiss-cheese model where "the individual 'finds a hole and keeps nibbling'" (Pearson, Shavlik, and Touchton 1989, 369). According to Carol Pearson and her colleagues, this approach to change recognizes the complexity of institutional systems, the challenges of initiating change from outside positions of authority, and the degree of self-knowledge and honesty required for institutional change. It requires experimenting with alternative ways of thinking and acting so that holes are created within the whole and the hold of old paradigms are loosened. As Pearson and her colleagues observe, "institutional change is more likely to happen rapidly in places prepared for change by effective nibblers" (370).

In the first chapter, I locate the debate about the function of the writing center in the larger cultural conflict between postmodernity and modernity. In the second chapter, I engage with critiques of postmodernity, particularly with its disregard of history, by locating writing center work within the historical contradictions of literacy, particularly the way that literacy teaching has been complicit in cultural regulation. In Chapter 3, I analyze the way that composition teaching regulates an academic identity, and I show how postmodern theories of subjectivity and agency can suggest ways to intervene in that regulation. In Chapter 4, I rethink the politics of writing center administration, applying Laclau and Mouffe's theory of articulatory politics to writing center issues. In the final chapter, I argue for a conception of fairness that holds writing center workers responsible not only for granting students membership to the academic literacy club but also for changing the gates of that club when change is necessary. In the afterword, Nancy Barron moves the discussion deeper into the debates about diversity, complicating commonsense understandings of difference, and suggesting some of the important work ahead of us.

Chapter One

P is for Postmodernity and for Possibilities

[P]ostmoderism . . . is the code name for the crisis of confidence in Western conceptual systems. It is borne out of the uprising of the ex-centrics, the revolution in communication technology, the fissures of a global multinational hyper-capitalism, and our sense of the limits of Enlightenment rationality, all creating a conjunction that shifts our sense of who we are and what is possible.
—Patti Lather, *Getting Smart*

Writing center workers are accustomed to seeing the university and its literacy practices from multiple perspectives. In the writing center, we encounter differences in worldviews, in cultural backgrounds, in educational histories, in teachers' expectations, and in disciplinary standards. We learn to stretch our conceptual horizons as we work with students who encounter academic expectations for the first time, students who are learning to write in unfamiliar genres, students whose academic work is affected by learning disabilities, or students whose literacies are not valued in the academy. The intellectual challenge of writing center work comes from having to entertain *both* the student's *and* the teacher's understandings simultaneously in ways that allow us to compassionately explain where these understandings collide and where the gaps occur.

Writing centers are often places where people develop what scholars call *postmodern skills:* the ability to simultaneously maintain multiple viewpoints, to make quick shifts in discourse orientation, to handle rapid changes in information technology, to work elbow to elbow with people differently positioned in the university hierarchy, to negotiate cultural and social differences, to handle the inevitable blurring of authorial boundaries, and to regularly renegotiate issues of knowledge, power, and ownership. This ability to work the border between tradition and change, to simultaneously entertain multiple—often conflicting—perspectives is a valuable survival skill for the turn of the century. Writing center work cultivates this mental agility, yet few people outside the writing center recognize this. In fact, writing center work is still often imagined as dull, sentence-level editing. Writing center people can get quite prickly about this negative representation, but in spite of many efforts to show the contrary, writing centers are considered to be backward places for students "with problems" or for students "who need help."

Attempts to change the impoverished representations of writing center work often result in frustration because the postmodernist understandings that develop in the writing center clash with the modernist understandings that structure higher education. In the postmodern encounters of a writing center, essential truths come under questioning, "reality" changes with a shift in perspective, one's identity shifts in response to different situations, and the coherence of an essay comes at the expense of complexity. Just as postmodernity pushes against the limits of modernist beliefs, so does writing center work expose the limits of existing literacy practices in higher education. But because writing centers are funded for modernist reasons (to improve the clarity, order, and correctness of student writing), writing center workers too often must avoid questioning taken-for-granted university assumptions in order to fulfill their designated function. Regardless of a student's class, country, or culture of origin, the university would like him or her to write, think, cite, and talk in clear, rational, coherent, Standard English.

If a student is not writing well, the problem, in moderist understandings, is presumed to lie with the student. Faculty are often relieved to have writing centers where they can "send" students to "get help" with their writing problems, but rarely are students happy to be sent to these places and to be identified as having problems. Taxpayers who willingly support community mental health services are not so willing to park their cars in the community mental health parking lot on the main road and confidently walk through the door because they "need help." Similarly, mental health workers are expected to concentrate on the individual's problem rather than suggest to educators, clergy members, police officers, physicians, or members of their own profession that their practices or beliefs are contributing to "the problem." Writing center directors, like myself, tend to be pragmatists. We make arguments for funding based on a modernist understanding of communication—the belief that truth can be communicated through clear, precise, transparent prose. Directly or indirectly, writing centers promise to help students achieve this clarity.

In this chapter and throughout this book, I suggest that modernist conceptions are reaching their limits. Within a modernist framework, writing centers will be chronically undervalued because they are expected to mask contradictions or contain differences. To rearticulate the value of the writing center, I argue for the possibilities offered by postmodern theorizing. The peril of this strategy is that by contrasting postmodern thinking with modernist thinking, I may seem to be elevating the postmodern over the modern, creating another binary with a privileged term, which is a very un-postmodern thing to do. I ask readers to remember that a good postmodern thinker must already be a modernist, particularly a modernist willing to recognize the limits of his or her theoretical frameworks. I use the term *postmodern* not to embrace any particular theory but instead as an acknowledgment of the change in human consciousness that has resulted from technological transformation in communication and transportation, increased encounters with diversity, and a global economy—all of which have dramatically increased our daily encounters with "radically discontinuous realities" (Jameson 1992, 413). Our efforts to negotiate these discontinuous and multidimensional realities frequently challenge us to realign our understandings about communication, identity, and politics.

My aim in this chapter is to show what writing centers might gain from the conceptual possibilities of postmodernity as well as to show how persistent modernist beliefs hold us back. Using a combination of theory, metaphor, story, and argument, I attempt to create a more complicated vision of writing center work. Like Patti Lather whose comment opens this chapter, I believe that the conceptual possibilities in postmodern theoretical formulations can be put to work to change practice and to help us rethink "our sense of who we are and what is possible"(1991, 159).

To illustrate the challenges faced by today's college graduates, I offer the examples of two recent college graduates in my family. Last year, my nephew's job in the computer software industry required him to maintain three separate residences—at the same time. He had an address and phone number in Los Angeles, Houston, and Chicago. A person with three addresses faces unusual challenges when called on to make decisions about where to vote and how to negotiate the responsibilities of friendships, family, and community. My daughter, an information systems specialist, works for a firm that manages corporate benefit packages. In five years, the firm's "campus" has added three multistory buildings, and my daughter has changed positions seven times. New projects require a quick reconfiguration of professional roles and priorities; they also require twelve-hour work days and logging in on weekends to do company problem solving. What kind of education prepares one for such work intensification? How does one negotiate the distinctions between company time and personal time?

From a modernist standpoint, the lifestyles of these two recent college graduates might be interpreted as their "not wanting to settle down," as challenges to family address books that have room for only one address and phone number, as a rejection of parental lifestyle, as indications of corporate excess, or as evidence of firstborn overachievement. But within a postmodern framework, these young people are negotiating social saturation and the complex challenges of a career in information technology. As Troy Duster observes, today's college graduates need to learn how "to get along in a future that will no longer be dominated by a single group spouting its own values as the ideal homogenized reality for everyone else" (1995, 283). Alternative career choices in fields that are not as technically saturated hardly offer enough salary for a single person to make rent payments and afford a reliable car.

In spite of these rapidly changing social conditions, universities still operate in much the same way as they did thirty years ago. Modernist beliefs in individual autonomy, rational thinking, and transparent communication structure the system. Faculty positions rarely change, curricular innovation is sluggish, the disciplines remain segmented, the closed classroom door protects the privacy of teaching, academic hierarchies prevail, the Library of Congress system demands a primary author, plagiarism remains the most serious of academic offenses, the existence of lecture halls supports an information-delivery model of education, and multiculturalism is imagined as curriculum revision rather than a long-ignored historical reality.

Many persistently unresolvable issues about writing center identity, function, and funding are connected to the university's necessary loyalty to modernist systems at this time of great cultural transition to postmodernity. Questions that emerge repeatedly in writing center conversations are connected to modernist assumptions about individual autonomy, ownership, and responsibility: Should we send faculty members reports on students? Should we let faculty know when we suspect a student of plagiarizing? Should writing center tutors be allowed to write on a student's paper? Are peer tutors really qualified for the job? How often and for how long should we allow a student to use the writing center? Should the director be tenure-track or professional staff? Modernity indirectly promises that we may find a right answer if we work at it long enough and hard enough. Personally, I don't think modernity is up to the task.

For a long time, composition teaching itself has clung to the notion of the autonomous individual. Lester Faigley summarizes the persistence of modernist assumptions in composition teaching:

> Where composition studies has proven least receptive to postmodern theory is in surrendering its belief in the writer as an autonomous self, even at a time when extensive group collaboration is practiced in many writing classrooms. Since the beginning of composition teaching in the late nineteenth century, college writing teachers have been heavily invested in the stability of the self and the attendant beliefs that writing can be a means of self-discovery and intellectual self-realization. (1992, 15)

In spite of an awareness that complicated topics are enriched when we bring multiple perspectives to them, teachers still would like students to write from a coherent and unified point of view. When writing problems occur, teachers are quick to locate them in individual students rather than in the contradictions inevitably encountered in complex topics, in the lack of acceptable student genres for engaging complexity, or in the problematic subjectivity invoked by the assignment.

When modernist assumptions about self-discovery and realization are accepted uncritically, the contradictions at the heart of writing center work are never addressed. Why, for example, are writing center tutors *not* supposed to write on students' papers yet the students' teachers *are* supposed to write on them? If teachers are allowed to write on students' papers, why do we say students should "own" their papers? Why are writing centers worried about "appropriating" students' texts when assignments require "appropriate" genres, "appropriate" citation styles, and "appropriate" supporting material? Why is the "best" writing center approach considered nondirective, especially when students come to writing centers seeking explicit advice? Why is collaboration such a buzz-word and plagiarism such a serious offense? Why is it often so rewarding to work with students in the writing center and so frustrating to deal with expectations of what writing centers should do? Why is writing center pedagogy called collaborative if its purpose is individualized instruction? Why are writing centers called student-centered environments if what they really do is enforce the teacher's or the university's values? Why are students so frequently depicted as lacking or needing something? What theory of knowledge does that depiction support?

The clash between the conceptual assumptions of modernity and the realities of writing center work create conditions that remind me of driving home from the university during a winter storm. In the Upper Peninsula (U.P.) of Michigan, winter is an especially challenging season because we are surrounded on three sides by Lake Superior, the largest freshwater lake in the world, and we are far enough north to pick up Arctic weather coming through Canada. The large lake surface produces additional lake-effect snow that adds to our storm systems, resulting in an average winter snowfall exceeding 250 inches. Lake-effect snow doesn't just fall vertically like rain but also swirls horizontally, as from a vortex, against my windshield. As the sky darkens, the snow-covered highway blurs into the horizon, easily confusing my orientation on a long-familiar road. Headlights of cars heading the opposite direction flash in my eyes. As cars in the other lane pass, they kick up clouds of snow that create momentary whiteout conditions. I must resist the urge to brake and drive on slowly, hoping my Subaru's taillights are still visible, willing my tightened stomach muscles and clenched hands on the wheel to relax.

Like the U.P., writing centers are peninsulas, extending deeply into the waters of contemporary culture. They are often the first place on campus to become aware of changes in student populations, such as an increase in nontraditional students or in students with learning disabilities; or to feel the effects of programmatic changes, such as new grading policies or the implementation of portfolio assessment. Writing center workers often know more of what is happening in classrooms and residence halls than deans and department heads. They hear about harassment incidents, racial taunting, and instructor breakdowns. Writing centers are not buffered by traditional university hierarchies or predictable practices but instead are open to whatever the weather brings. Writing centers rarely set their own syllabi; they generally have large turnovers in the staff each year; their budget line is vulnerable because they do not usually generate credit hours or grades or other traditional markers of university value; the reporting line for the position of the writing center director is often unclear.

Over the years, for example, the budget for the writing center that I direct has been moved from the Humanities Department to the Dean of the College of Sciences and Arts, to the Director of Special Academic Programs, back to the Dean's office, next to the Center for Teaching, Learning, and Faculty Development, and now to the Associate Provost's office. With each move, I find myself reporting to a person unfamiliar with the work of the writing center. Whenever I enter into conversation with a new colleague, I struggle to find ways of explaining the value of the writing center to a person whose view of education, knowledge, communication, and students has probably not been affected by writing center experience. Colleagues accustomed to attending to surface features of student writing and intimately familiar with the discourse practices of their particular disciplines have difficulty imagining how writing center work could be anything more than comma fixing. From their perspectives, students who don't follow their assignments are lazy, confused, stubborn, culturally deprived, or slow. To some of them, writing center work smacks of coddling, of not holding people responsible for their work.

When I encounter these assumptions, understandings that seem so clear, so vital, so essential in the familiar surroundings of the writing center become strange. I can use statistical evidence to prove to my new colleagues that regular use of our writing center has had a positive impact on retention. As handy as this evidence is, however, it doesn't take me into discussions that convey the intellectual work of the writing center. Like Helen Fox (1994), I would rather tell stories of writing center students that expose the limits of our academic perspectives, and like James Gee (1996), I would like to make the argument that many academic writing assignments regulate student subjectivity rather than promote cognitive or critical development. But moving into that kind of discussion is dangerous without adequate preparation. I am aware that if I offer an alternative perspective, particularly one that directs attention away from "students who need help" and toward teaching practices that can be made more motivating or tacit evaluation practices that can be made more explicit, I create dangerous conditions for the vulnerable writing center budget. My listeners may think I am simply making excuses for students. The disjuncture between what I know from writing center experience and what is imagined about the writing center creates whiteout conditions. To keep the writing center funded for next year, I must be careful to stay on my side of the road, or at the least be sure that my intentions and the direction of my argument are visible to others.

Over the years, I have learned how to prepare for winter storms. I drive an all-wheel drive vehicle; in whiteout conditions, I look for familiar landmarks on the sides of the highway to judge my bearings; I put heat-reflecting insoles in my boots; I wear polar fleece and down-filled jackets; I put my gloves away in November and wear thick mittens until spring. Just as I have located resources in my efforts to deal with winter, so I have located critical theories that enable me to understand the conflicts in the conceptual systems of modernity and postmodernity, theories that enable me to survive the stormy transition to postmodernism and to expand my repertoire of arguments about the function and value of the writing center.

Theorizing does not make the problems go away any more than my polar parka prevents winter from happening. But the parka does contribute to my readiness for winter, even to my enjoyment of winter's beauty as I walk the dog at night wrapped in windproof layers of down.

Winter teaches us to be prepared, to have our vehicles and homes and wardrobes ready for severe testing. Preparation does not prevent the storms; nor does it guarantee safe passage in blizzard conditions. But preparation creates the savvy, the awareness, and the camaraderie that gets us through winter, the long season between fall and spring.

Similarly, reading theory to reflect on writing center issues helps me achieve perspective on cultural change, perspective that allows me to think my way through conflicts in conceptual systems rather than simply react to them. Braking suddenly in whiteout conditions in a heavy snowstorm is a defensive response likely to cause a rear-end collision or a spinout on icy roads. One needs to keep on moving through the storm even when the horizon disappears. Because postmodernity, like winter, is inevitable, one is well advised to proceed cautiously and to be aware of its dangers and its opportunities. For me, theorizing works in the same way as the insoles, the mittens, the new tires that prepare me for winter.

Rearticulating writing center issues in a postmodern framework is a task that requires as much caution and care as does driving in a winter storm. In the U.P. we learn to drive slowly when the weather changes, to pay close attention to weather reports, to know when the plows have been pulled off the secondary roads, to have our cars equipped with emergency blankets, shovels, sand, coffee cans, and candles. We never leave the house without our boots, and we call ahead to let others know we're on our way. Sometimes we know it's best to just stay put, to let the storm pass. In the same way writing center work makes us intensely aware of the clashes between thought systems, and requires that we develop the skills to negotiate them.

For many years, writing centers have defined themselves in modernist terms as sites of individualized instruction that unequivocally support the teacher's position while showing students the kind of writing valued in the academy. To take advantage of postmodern possibilities, writing centers need to be particularly aware of the defensive patterns that block the potential for change. Because postmodern conditions undermine modernist beliefs about the freely choosing rational individual, the neutrality of academic literacy, and education as a progressive and liberating process, they erode rationales that are central to modernist educational paradigms and to writing centers themselves.

Defensive Responses to Postmodern Change

Traveling into such slippery and threatening territory raises defensive responses that can block the potential for change. When defensive responses become institutionalized in writing center theorizing, programming, and styles of argumentation, they get in the way of exploring alternative possibilities. If most of our conceptual energy is directed toward defending the role of the writing center, we miss opportunities to take persuasive positions around the limits of academic literacy in a writing center. One of the first moves toward a more positive interventionist role for writing centers is to disconnect from the defensive responses to postmodern change. Anyone who has had to cope with dramatic change will recognize these defenses because all of them are common psychological responses that occur on an individual as well as institutional level.

Distancing. When anxiety is high, people often try to distance themselves from the situation creating the anxiety. Although it is easy to perceive distancing as a sign of apathy and disengagement, it is more likely to occur when we care so much that the anxiety overwhelms our coping ability. When universities encounter students with unanticipated and complex differences, they often create "special" programs for these students, programs distanced from the main business of the institution. In the mid-1970s, when Michigan experienced the earliest sign of postmodernity—a shift from a manufacturing to an information- and service-driven economy—one of the university's first responses was to establish the *Language Skills Lab*. Students of urban working-class and rural farming families, who in previous generations did not attend college, now had to be assimilated into the system. Because their language and background marked them as different, the university sent them to this newly created remedial facility. This distancing occurred not because faculty didn't care, but rather because they cared a great deal about ensuring the academic success of this new and unfamiliar group of students.

The earliest version of our writing center was a laboratory filled with bulky tape players and headphones. Diagnostic "instruments" were used to determine which tapes and workbooks were most appropriate to a particular student's language deficiencies and, once a match was made, the student was sent off alone into the lab with these materials. In light of today's understandings, this approach lacked all the qualities we deem essential for the development of literacy, but in the mid-1970s, the faculty viewed it as a reasonable response to a changed student population. The original language laboratory evolved into a tutorial-based writing center, as did many other skill-and-drill writing centers across the country. Nevertheless, the work of the writing center remained distanced from the mainstream business of the university.

Because faculty distanced themselves from social change by the very programs they established to manage change—writing centers, at-risk programs, equal opportunity programs—curriculum and teaching

methods quickly become out of sync with the changing student population. Serious gaps between the rhetoric of inclusion and the actual
conditions belie the appearance that the university has included a new
constituency. As compositionist Alice Roy observes, students of difference, while being "included. . . are not invited to invent a new university that might suit them, and possibly the mainstream, better" (1995,
186). Special programs are often staffed by part-time faculty or by professional staff who claim that their work with students from linguistically and culturally diverse backgrounds has transformed their teaching. However, this personal transformation is not usually documented
or theorized in ways that influence faculty. There are some exceptions.
For example, Anne DiPardo and Helen Fox have offered richly textured
accounts of their work with nonmainstream students. Unfortunately
this work tends to be read and appreciated by those who teach and tutor in programs designed for nonmainstream students.

The contradictory situation whereby universities establish writing centers, then repeatedly question their value is connected to this
distancing mechanism, and writing centers themselves contribute to
the situation. Often, writing centers inadvertently distance themselves
from the academic work of the university by representing writing centers as places where students can find refuge, comfort, and support.
These representations gloss over the identity struggles that students experience in literacy learning and ignore the gatekeeping function of literacy. On the other hand, many writing centers distance themselves
from a remedial classification by promoting writing centers as places for
all writers, *not just* remedial writers. The *not just* qualifier was a defensive response to the lack of recognition accorded those who work in
writing centers. Thus, the increased diversity of students in higher education is avoided twice—first by universities establishing programs
like writing centers that distance faculty from students; and second by
writing centers' distancing themselves from a remedial function. Con-
sequently, the understandings and experiences that diverse students
bring to the university are rarely integrated into the mainstream business of the institution.

Blaming. When I first started making those white-knuckle winter
drives, I occasionally entertained thoughts of blame toward my husband
because it was his decision to accept a position at a university located in
the Upper Peninsula. However, blaming only delayed my adjustment
from living in easy-winter Oklahoma to living in nine-months-of-
winter Upper Michigan. When one encounters the multiple realities of
the postmodern condition, one is inclined to defend one's own reality
by blaming others. Blaming imposes a mechanistic cause-and-effect
relationship on human interactions. We construct negative representa-

tions of the other person or group, and when anxiety is heightened, we triangulate by seeking a sympathetic audience for those representations.

Because the university is so strongly tied to modernist beliefs in individualism and education as progressive, there is often a lot of blame circulating when change accelerates. Highly educated, keenly individualistic people who take pride in their rational observations are likely to point fingers elsewhere when budgets are lean, when governance breaks down, when enrollments change, when programs are cut, when students do not meet expectations. Faculty blame the writing center when student papers aren't what they expect them to be; writing centers blame faculty when they are misrepresented; and students blame writing centers when their papers don't meet the instructor's approval.

The blaming mechanism is deeply connected to the modernist belief in individual responsibility. If teachers are fulfilling their responsibilities (preparing for class, writing copious comments on students' papers, carefully considering text selection and assignment sequence), and students still do poorly, then surely it must be because students fail to take responsibility. Sometimes students are irresponsible, but more often the problem is in a breakdown of understanding about the complexities of the responsibility, a tendency to ignore the "response" in responsibility, or a tendency to see responsibilities as externally derived rather than located in the interaction between two people. Blame is an effective defense because it protects us from examining our own implications in a problem. We blame others rather than shift perspective when someone (particularly a student) offers a different version of reality.

In a study of the history of composition, Susan Miller traces the habit of blaming students back to an early report on student writing by the Harvard Board of Overseers in 1865. She observes that "the grotesqueries of [student] handwriting and of paragraphing" were "gleefully found and reported with the sympathy and understanding we might expect of young boys looking at a circus fat lady" (1991, 55). Representing students as objects of derision, as spectacle, persists well into this century. Marguerite Helmers' (1994) recent book-length study of testimonials in composition journals shows that teachers construct students as stock characters, lacking in agency, skill, knowledge, requisite attitudes, insight, and ability.

Writing center workers can be just as likely to blame students as faculty members are. They blame students for waiting until the last minute, for not having the right priorities, for not taking writing seriously, for wanting more from the writing center (proofreading? editing? conversational practice?) than the writing center is prepared to give. Blame shields us from scrutinizing our implication in inadequate schooling, prohibits questioning of academic pretensions, and limits us to narrow monocultural views. Worse yet, blame erects formidable psychological barriers for students from different racial, cultural, and class backgrounds.

Helping the other become more like us. A third common defensive reaction to social change is an effort to keep things the same, to make the present more like the past, to help the Other read and write more like the mainstream. Writing centers are particularly implicated in this reaction because so many writing centers were developed by people influenced by the liberal sympathies of the late 1960s and early 1970s. These reformers (I was one of them) were motivated by an egalitarian narrative, and they were determined to make it possible for previously excluded populations to succeed in college. We still believed the modernist narrative of education as progressive and liberating, so rather than rethink education, we sought to help the Other become like us. In theorizing peer tutoring, Kenneth Bruffee explained that tutoring programs were structured to "create and maintain the sorts of social contexts, the sorts of community life, that foster the kinds of conversation we value" (1984, 6). When peer tutoring is conceptualized as an effort to help students "loosen ties to the knowledge community they currently belong to and join another" (12), it doesn't take into account that students live in multiple communities with competing interests and values, that the values of communities can be in profound conflict, and that communities rarely keep their doors open for people to enter at will. As Alice Gillam observes, such efforts to theorize tutoring are "idealized, unproblematic, and acontextual" (1994, 39) or, in other words, quite ineffectual in guiding practice. That kind of theorizing may serve as a rallying point for writing center directors, but rarely does it touch practice in useful ways.

Even though educators increasingly encounter students who do not share their cultural values and mental models, they still expect students to somehow magically become more like them. Those of us who belong to a dominant class and culture and who see that culture reflected back to us in media representations tend to forget that we "have" culture. Whiteness and Anglo values are perceived as transparent, as normal, as universally desired, rather than as deriving from a culture. Those of us who are mainstream prefer communication with those who share our mental models. We don't have the patience required when someone doesn't "get" our point quickly or takes too long to "get to the point." Thinking that clear communication can be achieved through the use of Standard English and rationally structured arguments, we forget that our particular literacy patterns also carry our deeply held notions of what is polite, what is sophisticated, what is good, and what is valuable. We tend to think of students who use language differently as being inexperienced or mistaken or suffering from dialect or native-language "interference." Regarding just one of those language differences—the American academic preference for direct communication style—Helen Fox reminds us that "the indirect strategies of world-majority students are not the result of inexperience or confusion, but of training and purpose, for they have been brought up to value a subtle or roundabout communication style as polite and sophisticated" (1994, 14). Reading Fox, I wonder whether the international students who visit our writing center are amused or exasperated by our persistent efforts to teach them to write in ways they find rude and unsophisticated.

Helping (or, more realistically, expecting) the Other to become like us also makes teachers and tutors the heroes in the narrative of outreach—literacy missionaries rather than literacy maids. David Bartholomae observes that the metaphor of development underlying the philosophy of many basic writing programs allows us to think of students as immature writers. In this way, we avoid confronting the ways that academic literacy reproduces and reinforces divisions of race, class, and culture. When we encounter writing that we "are not prepared to read" (1993, 12), we define it as a student problem rather than our own reading problem. Bartholomae comments on this "telling irony" on his campus, "where young working-class women write, scholars go to archives to 'discover' working-class writing by women" (17).

Bartholomae locates the problem in modernist discourse. He observes, "the profession has not been able to think beyond an either/or formulation—either academic discourse or the discourse of the community; either argument or narrative; either imitation or expression" (19). Too often, decisions about programs for students who struggle with academic discourse rely on what Bartholomae calls "an established and corrupt discourse of 'boneheads,' of 'true college material,' of 'remediation'" (20). Rather than support the tidy distinctions of modernism, Bartholomae argues for a change in the way the profession talks about students who don't fit. This includes developing "a theory of error that makes the contact between the conventional and unconventional discourse the most interesting and productive moment for a writer or for a writing course" (1993, 19).

For nonmainstream writers *and* for mainstream writers, this point of contact often occurs in writing centers. Writing centers are uniquely situated to begin offering more complicated representations of students; representations that change the way we talk about students—not as incomplete and undeveloped individuals "who need our help," but as complicated people with history, class, and culture. Rather than being places where errors are fixed and differences are erased or where students find refuge and support, writing centers can be places where students learn to negotiate and understand the contact and conflicts of differences. Rather than helping the Other become more like us, the work of the writing center might instead include developing the ability to see ourselves as the Other, to recognize the limits of our worldviews and our cultural assumptions and to regard our discursive practices from the perspectives of those outside the mainstream discourse.

Conceptual Possibilities of Postmodern Thinking

Practitioners may still question the relevance of theoretical discussions about postmodernity when writing centers are so challenged by the ongoing conditions of modernity—revered university hierarchies, persistent concern about tutoring's threat to the notion of solitary authorship, and stubborn misunderstandings about the role of students in higher education. Smart practitioners are likely to ask just how theorizing about postmodernity will solve the problems they encounter in their administrative work, problems such as the need to do more with less, assessment pressures, stagnant budgets, the yearly challenge of hiring and training new tutors, the crush of students during finals week, the unfilled schedule early in the term, and the debate about whether to start an on-line writing center. If theorizing solved these problems, I would not be awake at 3 A.M. sipping on a mug of Sleepytime Tea in an attempt to calm my chattering mind. Theorizing doesn't help me sleep better, and it doesn't substitute for long problem-solving discussions with students, friends, colleagues, and mentors. Nor does it replace necessary efforts to cultivate good relationships with other units and administrators on campus. But the search for theoretical understanding does offer me new arguments and perspectives for resolving problems; because theorizing feeds my intellectual understanding and suggests alternatives, it prevents despair.

Thinking in postmodern frameworks allows me to develop proactive rather than reactive responses, to stand outside familiar thought systems, and to imagine alternative ways of responding to change. In the following section, I use stories about three writing center students to illustrate the ways postmodern thinking helps me change the terms of the argument rather than stay stuck in defensive positions. Postmodern thinking is not a panacea, but because it suggests different moves, different questions, and different interpretations, it allows me to articulate the already postmodern nature of writing center work.

To illustrate the possibilities of postmodern thinking, I borrow heavily from a hopeful vision of the postmodern articulated by Kenneth Gergen in *The Saturated Self* (1991), a book that translates the cultural shifts of postmodernity into everyday language. Gergen finds hopefulness in the postmodern willingness to question three problematic tenets of modernism—progress, individualism, and totalizing discourse.

Progress? According to Gergen, the Western concept of progress is not so much an observable phenomenon as it is a modernist narrative form. He observes,

> The enchantment of modernism derives importantly from its promise of progress—the belief that, with proper application of reason and ob- servation, the essences of the natural world may be made increasingly known, and that with such increments in knowledge the society may move steadily toward a utopian state. (232)

Gergen calls the narrative of progress a powerful "linguistic pose" that calls others to assent to our meaning system. To a postmodern thinker like Gergen, progress "can be seen as a form of secular religion, as a societal addiction, or as a rationalization for exploitation" (236). The narrative of progress sets up a game that "lays the foundation for a social hierarchy." Such games are, naturally, "most favored by those in a position to win them" (236).

Postmodernism disrupts the narrative of progress by calling atten- tion to what the narrative excludes. It examines tales of progress from multiple perspectives, asking whose voices are included and who stands to benefit and who stands to lose from accepting a particular view. In the writing center, postmodernism invites me to adopt an ecological perspective on what is called progress. Instead of looking only at stu- dent writing or students' grades for evidence of progress, I can instead ask how well the university accommodates students from economic, cultural, educational, and religious backgrounds that are outside the mainstream. I can also ask if writing center work is impacting teaching practices or contributing to changes in the curriculum. This broader perspective does not mean that the writing center no longer supports students' academic progress, but that I think in more complicated and integrated ways about what counts as progress.

To illustrate, I offer the example of Joe, an engineering student who worked in our writing center several years ago. Like many of our students, Joe was from a rural area, and he readily admitted to being more comfortable in the woods than in the classroom or the writing center. Quiet, easy-going, agreeable, and a man of few words, Joe worked with the most experienced writing coach on the staff during his enrollment in his first-year writing courses. As part of a small re- search project, his writing center sessions were taped and studied, and I interviewed Joe and his writing coach after he completed the course.[1] His teacher, an experienced graduate teaching assistant, was using John

Gage's text, *The Shape of Reason* (1987), which takes a rhetorical approach to argumentation, inviting students "to confront real intellectual problems needing real solutions," and to "write seriously about
ideas that require their serious attention" (v).

With his coach's help, Joe managed to earn an A in his course—a
sign of real progress to a modernist. But a postmodernist would ask
what Joe did to earn an A. Although Joe wrote an analysis of the pub-
licity tactics used by animal rights activists, he never once revealed his
identity as the son and grandson of mink farmers, nor did he attempt
to explain what it means to earn a living in a way that is often under
attack in the popular press. When I interviewed Joe after the course, he
did not volunteer information about his background. When I asked
him what he had learned in the course, he told me that he had learned
to write from facts and to keep personal bias out of his papers. Near the
end of the interview, I indicated that his writing coach had told me
about his experience on the mink farm and that I was interested in
hearing more about it. As he talked about life on the farm, the hesi-
tancy and struggle to find words that were apparent earlier in the interview and on many of the videotapes disappeared. He spoke of his
family's decision to earn their living this way so that they could raise
their children in a rural area. He spoke of his chores on the farm and of
the mink who slept all day except when Joe came by with the food cart.
The conditions on the farm, he said, were not at all like those depicted
in the popular press. He talked of his brother, a student at another college, who was writing about the history of trapping in the northern
Great Lakes region and of his family's interest in his initial research,
their offers to send him publications produced by the association of
mink farmers.

What happened to this knowledge? At some point in the term, Joe's
instructor warned him on a draft to "Watch out for bias." Joe's concern
about bias developed into the problem of how to include his own experience in what is supposed to be a well-reasoned library research paper.
In one of his writing center sessions, Joe explained to his writing coach
that the conditions the activists say exist on the farms couldn't be true
because underfed and crowded mink do not produce good pelts. (His
hand stroked an imaginary mink as he spoke.) He described the mink
yard—the sleeping mink who wake only when the food cart comes—
and he explained that when activists release mink, they disrupt a natural balance. The mink either starve or cause disruption on a nearby
chicken farm.

The following transcript of one of Joe's writing center sessions reveals his frustration with the task of writing a thesis statement that
clarifies his position *and* allows him to integrate what he knows with
what he has read. In response to his writing coach's question about

what he thought he had to do next, Joe pointed to a sentence his instructor had underlined and replied:

> I suppose I should have to expand on that or something. I need to try
> . . . to show that fur farming . . . that activists don't . . . aren't really . . .
> I don't know (*laughs*). I'll have to think about that—um (*long pause*).
> Well this should . . . you know . . . I could just take . . . well because . . .
> there is a lot of . . . I try to show by the—the way they go about. . . .
> You know the way they . . . how they treat people and how their tac-
> tics are . . . for demonstrating and that along with all the, yeah, mis-
> conceptions . . . spread by them that the fur farms, they say are, you
> know . . . I don't know. (*Smiles*). That's why I'm having trouble stating
> what . . .

Joe knew that the way the activists depicted businesses like his family's in news accounts did not correspond to what he knew from his experience. Mike Rose writes about this phenomenon: "Having crossed boundaries, you sometimes can't articulate what you know, or what you know seems strange" (1989, 241).

The writing coach put Joe's struggle into words and explained how to write a thesis. She suggested strategies for development and encouraged Joe to talk with his teacher. Joe, however, decided to exclude his personal experience and to shift his focus. His performance in the course was rewarded with an A. He had learned what Linda Brodkey calls the fluency trick: "write a thesis statement simple enough that it can *appear* to be adequately elaborated and naturally resolved in the requisite number of words" (1995, 222). As Brodkey explains, in order to please the teacher with a display of verbal fluency, "successful" student writers learn to ignore the complexity of topics.

Joe completed the composition sequence without a sense of how his experience might count as evidence, without having contributed to anyone's understanding of life as a mink farmer, without a voice confident enough to speak about what he knew in academic circles, and without having produced a piece of writing he felt was worth keeping. Although his parents had requested a copy of his paper, he said that he had never bothered bringing his essay home. In fact, he wasn't sure if he kept the final paper. The "withouts" are not due to a lack of effort on Joe's part or his teacher's or his writing coach's but to a lack within the modernist conception of composition, a lack of attention to writing about issues that are not covered in the popular press, and a lack of argumentative forms that can allow for the complicated and contradictory inclusion of experience that written materials do not confirm. The modernist genre of the research paper might work for students whose experience is mainstream, but for students like Joe (who certainly *appears* to be mainstream), we need more complicated, flexible forms that encourage writers to explore the contradictions between private experience and public knowledge. At the very least, we need opportunities for students like Joe to explain how their experience does not conform to or somehow exceeds the container. Perhaps rather than grading students on the final performance of a seamless paper, we might instead grade them on the insights they develop—about how experience can exceed or contradict a given genre; about the responses they consider when they encounter the disjunctures; about the time they anticipate it might take to resolve the issues; about the tactics they used in the absence of adequate time; and about the consequences of those tactics.

Postmodern thinking would move writing centers beyond helping students fit their experience into tidy genres and into dialogue with faculty about how the teaching of composition can be transformed so that students like Joe can produce writing that he, his family, and his instructor would all value. I do not imagine a scenario where writing coaches would be bustling into faculty offices every time a student confronted a contradiction. Instead I imagine, in addition to celebrating progress in terms of student visits and student grades, that writing centers will become places where deeply reflective analysis can happen, where students and teachers can periodically join us in questioning the status quo and exploring the inadequacies of our modernist genres and pedagogies so that we can move toward more complicated understandings of what it means to teach and learn literacy in postmodern times.

Individualism? If writing centers across the country have any one theoretical underpinning in common, it is the emphasis on individualized instruction. The one-to-one relationship is often thought to be the most important contributor to writing center effectiveness because one knowledgeable tutor is able to address one student at a time. Within a modernist framework, individualized instruction is generally considered a good, relatively innocent activity, and writing center directors feel quite secure in representing their work to faculty by celebrating the value of working one-to-one. That is, they feel secure until questions are raised about whether a tutor is being too directive or about how carefully a tutor is observing the teacher's agenda or about how much of the work is truly "the student's own" or about how the results of individualized instruction should be evaluated. These questions have generated a great deal of writing center scholarship that attempts to qualify the kind of collaboration that occurs in writing centers or to address the ethics of writing center practice. Many writing centers have developed codes of behavior to ensure individual autonomy: a tutor is *not* supposed to tell a student what to do, a tutor is *not* supposed to hold the pen, a tutor is *not* supposed to undermine a teacher by giving conflicting advice, a tutor is *not* supposed to proofread for a student. The rules are intended to safeguard individual agency even when they may interfere with effectiveness. The paradoxical situation whereby individualized instruction is a good thing that can readily become *too* good rests on the modernist belief that the individual is the one who knows, the one who chooses, the one who is responsible. Gergen observes that the American belief in the individual as the wellspring of human action is "both peculiarly Western and historically perishable" (1991, 239). Nevertheless, this concern for individual autonomy insinuates itself into many suspicions about the efficacy of writing center work.

We forget that the Western focus on the individual is also the basis for social hierarchies, for annual cultural rituals such as player-of-the-year award or teacher-of-the-year award. Such rituals elevate one individual over all others, ignore the complex interdependency underlying good work, and create competitive rather than cooperative relationships. The "rhetorical power" of terms such as "individual rights," "autonomy," and "personal worth" acts as a "barrier to critical scrutiny" (Gergen 1991, 240). Numerous social researchers including Robert Bellah, Christopher Lasch, and Richard Sennett have concluded that our emphasis on individualism has trivialized relationships and interfered with the development of commitment at every level of society.

Although the postmodern shift to a fragmented and multiple self has caused consternation for many modernists, Gergen finds hope in the shift from a focus on the individual as the center of reality to a concept of a relational reality that accounts for human interconnectedness. He reminds us that meanings are determined by relationships: "My words don't become 'communication' until they are treated by others as intelligible . . . [M]eaning is not the product of individual minds but of relationship" (242–43). Gergen comments that one of the simplest human gestures, the handshake, has no meaning unless it is reciprocated.

In the writing center, an emphasis on relationship rather than individualized instruction allows me to leave behind defensive concerns about how much help is too much and whether the tutor is adequately enacting the teacher's desires. Instead I can keep the focus on the ways the writing center supports students' efforts to enter into relationship with academic values, disciplinary texts, mainstream literacy. I can remember that literacy is the achievement of a relationship with other minds, with a culture's texts, and with a discipline. Many accounts of those who have successfully crossed boundaries from one literacy to another are stories of important relationships, of people who removed hidden barriers by making the tacit explicit and who were willing to rethink their own belief system in an effort to clarify their relationships with others. These understandings provide better guideposts for responsible action in a tutoring situation than constant exhortations about what *not* to do.

A postmodern framework also encourages me to think of students not as isolated individuals but as members of communities and families. To illustrate how this relational focus changes the ways in which I articulate the value of writing center work, I offer the example of Patty, a student who worked in our writing center several years ago.[2] Patty has multiple learning disabilities and a hearing impairment that affects her speech; she arrived at our writing center with an educational history that included years of verbal taunting by peers, the disregard of teachers, a delayed high school graduation, and academic dismissal from a less competitive university than ours. Her personal history included the hardships of family poverty, ill health, unplanned pregnancy, and single parenthood. If it had not been for Patty's strong family support system, particularly her mother's belief in her intelligence, Patty's self-esteem would have been irreparably damaged by school. Patty's voice, affected by her hearing impairment, is loud and monotone, and her social skills are unsophisticated. In the open environment of our writing center, it was hard to concentrate on sessions with other students because of the "distraction" that Patty's differences created.

Few teachers would question that Patty deserved individual attention, but as the modernist director of our busy writing center, I did question whether Patty deserved a more generous allocation of time than other students. Patty was not a good fit at our competitive university, so was it "fair" to allow her more "help" than other students? Was it "fair" to allocate extra time to Patty if that meant less time available to students who were a better fit at the university? How would our "success" with Patty be determined? Was it enough to hope that she would pass the course? Was that fair to her? Did we have the expertise to address her needs? How did it happen that a student with so many educational challenges was admitted to this competitive university? Was it up to us to provide her with as much help as we saw fit or were we open to challenge on that issue? To whom would we have to explain ourselves? What did her daily presence in the center communicate to other students? Modernist thinking too easily supports a concept of fairness that distributes goods according to "policy" rather than according to one individual's need in relationship to others'.

As it turned out, a coincidence moved us beyond these administrative concerns. A graduate student on the staff returned from study at another university during the middle of the term, and his unfilled schedule and interest in Patty resolved some of the problems. When I review that situation through a postmodern lens, I can see that our "success" with Patty had less to do with individualized instruction and more to do with the expanded relationships we developed as a result of her writing coach's suggestions. He coordinated a time for our staff to meet with Patty's vocational rehabilitation counselor, and as a consequence we began to think about the writing center's role in community efforts for people with disabilities. In time, the artwork of Patty's daughter, Crystal, decorated my office door, and the entire writing center staff came to know Patty's mother, Romance, who was also a student at the university and a frequent writing center visitor. We shared Patty's grief at her mother's untimely death the following year and were deeply touched by Patty's thank-you card. Most important, this expanded network provided more than good feelings. It changed Patty's relationship to educational institutions, and it changed our writing center's relationship with students like Patty. Our newly established connection with community resources, our changed thinking about working with students with disabilities, and our entrance into multiple relationships did more to support Patty than any single one-to-one session. Moreover, these changed relationships resulted in gains for students that followed Patty.

A good modernist would ask: did Patty's writing improve enough to pass the course? Can Patty now "write on her own"? A postmodern answer casts the net deeper. Patty's self-confidence had been damaged by educational institutions; we had taken some small steps to shore it up, and in the process we learned to question the practices of schooling. We established a cooperative relationship with the vocational rehabilitation counselor, and she made us aware of community resources for university students with learning disabilities; the writing center staff made strides in individual ability to interact with differences; and the scholarship of the writing coach who worked with Patty was profoundly affected by this encounter. In summary, our success should not be measured by Patty's individual achievement but by how much the writing center and its staff (and ultimately the university) gained from our interactions with her. Does this mean the writing center gained at Patty's expense? Patty was aware that her work with us would support the students who followed her. I believe that in the writing center she felt accepted as an adult who had something to offer rather than as a problem needing to be fixed. Our writing center did provide Patty with individualized instruction, but the value of that work is more fully articulated when we think of it in relational terms. If we approach writing center work with the aim of understanding the ways we have all been constructed by the expectations of schooled literacy, we create more productive sites for relational learning.

Totalizing discourse? Gergen calls modernism a *totalizing discourse,* one that is insulated from criticism and locked into a singular perceptual world. Modernist beliefs tend to cohere into a systematized conceptual system that denies alternative realities. For example, a modernist framework links progressive accounts of schooling with the presumed neutrality of autonomous literacy and with the social belief that if one learns the values of academic literacy, one can surpass boundaries of race, ethnicity, disability, and class. When conventional beliefs, conventional practices, and conventional theories cohere into a system of thought, it becomes nearly impossible to doubt the status quo. Within such a system, the innocence of writing center practices is guaranteed. Writing center workers are often attracted to their work because they enjoy "helping others." They feel good, so they are unlikely to question the conceptual system that structures what they do. They are more likely to question the students who do not respond appropriately to their helpful suggestions.

The belief in the innocence of literacy work persists in spite of many literacy researchers who have proven it false. In a summary of this research, Harvey Graff observes that literacy is not the *cure for* but the *result of* economic, cultural, and social conditions (1991a, 377–78). Giving up belief in the literacy myth means facing the possibility that writing center work reproduces social divisions and unjustly regulates access and subjectivity. Gergen observes that modernists protect themselves from a loss of innocence by avoiding contact with those who seem moved by forces beyond reason, including the devoutly religious, the eccentrics, and the mentally impaired (1991, 246).

Postmodernism, on the other hand, reminds us that all claims to truth are grounded in specific discourses that favor some over others and that individuals hold tightly to their beliefs because of what the beliefs do for them not because they have a greater claim to truth than others. Political theorist Jane Flax reminds us that from a postmodern perspective "there is no way to test whether one story is closer to the truth than another because there is no transcendental standpoint or mind unencumbered by its own language and stories" (1993, 139). Postmodernism opens to the free play of discourse, to Bakhtin's heteroglossia, to a multiplicity of voices. Outside the totalizing discourse of modernism, Gergen observes

> There is little reason to suppress any voice. Rather, with each new vocabulary or form of expression, one appropriates the world in a different way, sensing aspects of existence in one that are hidden or absent in another, opening capacities for relatedness in one modality that are otherwise hindered. (1991, 247)

The postmodern emphasis on multiple discourses does not mean that modernist beliefs are abandoned but that they are held as potentials rather than absolute truths, as historical and cultural forms rather than products of superior reasoning. A postmodern orientation invites us to learn from alternate ways of naming the world. It offers increased opportunities for cultural renewal and critique, allowing us to incorporate the possibilities inherent in other cultures, and expanding our options for relating.

To illustrate the advantage of working outside the totalizing discourse of modernism in the writing center, I offer the story of Mary, a student who arrived at our writing center one busy afternoon during walk-in hours.[3] On the surface, Mary appeared to fit in easily with the small percentage of female students on campus—long blond hair, jeans, parka, a backpack slung over her shoulder. Her difference revealed itself in her unusual prose, which was saturated with biblical rhythms and overlaid with religious beliefs that seem strange in the academic world. She wrote about how she and her fiancé were yoked together by God such that they would bear each other's burdens and about how the sufferings and joys they would experience in marriage were part of God's plan for them. The beliefs expressed in her paper seemed not only unusual for a late-twentieth-century student, but also incongruent in a college essay.

Fortunately, the writing coach on duty was familiar with the beliefs and practices of several local religious communities and wondered if perhaps Mary was a member of one of them. She knew that these communities were not in the habit of questioning the authority of texts or the value of a single powerful perspective. Many of the members raised large families in homes without televisions, and they avoided movie theaters. Here was Mary in a cultural studies-based composition class investigating popular culture. Given that walk-in hours were busy and other students waited in line, the writing coach wondered what to do. Was she supposed to tell Mary to find another topic? recommend that she take a critical stance toward her beliefs, drawing on the feminist essays in her anthology? speculate about how Mary's peers and instructors will respond to her essay? unpack the tacit values that will influence an evaluation of her essay? tell Mary to come back at another time?

Postmodern thinking provides no easy answers to these questions, but it does hold in check our assumptions about the neutrality of the critical stance expected in academic discourse. Within a postmodern framework, we are more likely to proceed cautiously, aware that Mary's discourse carries a worldview that stands in contrast to the academic view and that the academic view is not necessarily more "right" than Mary's. We might respectfully juxtapose our worldview with hers, inviting her to tell us what ours offers and what it takes away. We might make an effort to learn more about the literacy practices of her community and use that knowledge to think about the writing program's interactions with students from a religious community whose languages, practices, and dispositions are very unlike those in circulation at the university. With the composition faculty, we might begin to imagine how students from that community can read and write in our courses in ways that respect their ties to a religious identity.

Within a postmodern framework, the writing center approaches Mary as a member of a community and wonders what we can learn about academic discourse from her perspective. We think not about replacing Mary's "inferior" understandings with "superior" ones, but instead invite her into a dialogue in which "subcultures may benefit from the discourses of their neighbors" (Gergen 1991, 250). Rather than sending us to institutional policy statements, postmodernism moves us into "direct interchange with the other." During these encounters, we should ask ourselves "What is the worldview within which their actions are intelligible and good? What place do we hold in that worldview? How do they perceive our view and their place within it?" (257). Freed from totalizing discourse, we are encouraged to explore alternate realities. In place of secure belief in the neutrality of academic literacy, we learn to take responsibility for the ways we are constituted by our social positions and histories and we learn to listen and to withhold judgment. Rather than hold tightly to perceptions of right and wrong, we become aware of how "reality" changes when our perceptions shift. We must develop, simultaneously, ways to live and work with painful ambivalence.

In a modernist world, students like Mary, who depart from our dominant cultural norm, must often assume unfamiliar identities or subjectivities in order to meet academic expectations. To say that we are helping these individuals in writing conferences erases the historical contingencies that position some of us as helpers of Others, masks the power relations involved, and positions students as needing our beneficence. Postmodern thinking does not challenge writing center efforts to support students like Mary but rather insists that we be more aware and honest about the tacit values operating in any particular approach to composition teaching. Postmodern thinking encourages us to engage with Mary's prose in ways that acknowledge her allegiance to a religious community; it challenges us to learn more about the literacies and cultural worldviews of students like Mary so that when we meet them in the writing center, we understand the discourses they use to construe their relationships with us, with texts, and with readers.

Our work with Mary and students like her can start with frank, respectful discussions of the ways their theories of the world contrast with our own. Additionally, we can refuse to essentialize students like Mary by recognizing that even though the formal discourse Mary knows from her experience of church relationships seems the most appropriate choice to her in the formal academic setting, it is probably not the only discourse she has available to her. With her help, a writing center coach can learn to juxtapose this authoritative discourse with academic discourses and to talk explicitly about the values encoded in academic discourse so that Mary and students like her can make informed choices. With them we can begin to develop new rhetorical skills— ways to call attention to a chosen stance—while acknowledging the expectations and assumptions of others. We can begin to imagine ways for Mary to write successfully in composition class without also imagining a need to weaken her ties to her ethnoreligious identity. We can invite Mary to help us understand what counts as educational progress.

Outsiders wonder why we endure the extreme winters in the Upper Peninsula of Michigan, and in the middle of hazardous winter drives, I wonder myself. But the winter storms recede from memory in the summer when I watch the sun rise over Lake Superior and, later in the day, gaze at the colors playing on the water at sundown. Reframing writing center issues in postmodern terms offers no easy road into the future, but it does offer opportunities to delve into previously suppressed conflicts in search of new understandings, new responses, and new ways of representing the writing center's value. It does so by asking us as Lather (1991) says, "[to shift] our sense of who we are and what is possible"—to refashion our assumptions. A writing center practice that articulates the efforts to educate an increasingly diverse student population can use that diversity to reveal the limitations of our worldviews and to intervene in the naturalized, mainstream literacy expectations that reproduce social hierarchies and limit agency. Postmodern thinking also makes it possible to develop a vision of a healthy mutual interdependence between the writing center and the classroom, an expanded sensitivity to "the network of relations in which we all participate" (Gergen 1991, 245). Within a postmodern framework, we can articulate the value of the writing center according to how well it contributes to institutional performance by increasing the spaces for listening; how much it contributes to understanding of difference; how often it creates participant roles for students; and how frequently and effectively it offers opportunities for faculty to understand the mental models that students bring to college.

From a postmodern perspective, writing centers are necessary spaces for the critical orientation and contextualization that fosters real learning. In a social setting saturated with contested meanings and values (like a university campus), both faculty and students need a space where values can be identified and discussed—where one can orient oneself or, in Jameson's (1992) terms, construct a cognitive map. Gergen writes that the postmodern invitation is to "carry the clown on one's shoulders—to always be ready to step out of 'serious character' and locate its pretensions, to parody or ape oneself" (1991, 193). Academics, rarely known for their sense of humor, do not find it easy to step out of serious character. Yet writing center work regularly invites us to hold the mirror up close, to see the inadequacies, the pretensions, the wrinkles of practices that previously looked smooth. In a postmodern culture, we need the ability to shift perspective, to simultaneously entertain multiple points of view. This regular shifting loosens our loyalty to monocultural values. When previously unintelligible perspectives come into focus, we shift away from defensive responses and instead search for more complicated understandings of literacy learning.

Notes

1. For this story, I am indebted to Joe, who agreed to have his sessions taped; to the members of the MTU Writing Center Research Group who studied the tapes with me; and to Jean Blanning, who was Joe's writing coach.

2. Much of what I have learned from thinking about our writing center's work with Patty is the result of the intellectual courage and persistence of Tim Fountaine. Tim was the graduate student writing coach who worked with Patty and who regularly invited our reflection on his work with her.

3. I am indebted to Marsha Penti's account of her work with Mary for this story. Marsha was the coach on duty the day Mary came to the writing center. Marsha reflected on this encounter during our weekly meetings and subsequently wrote about it for a conference paper. Her dissertation was motivated by this encounter.

Chapter Two

Literacy Learning in Postmodern Times
Coming to Terms with a Loss of Innocence

*a literacy adequate to a radical, heterogeneous democracy might
need to be driven neither by a normative identity nor a performative
political idea, but by the principle and skills of cultural translation,
the ability to negotiate across incommensurable traditions.*
— James Donald, "Literacy
and the Limits of Democracy"

We didn't have a campus writing center when I went to college, but I
was fortunate to have a smart friend down the hall in my dorm who
was willing to read my late-night drafts and who would ask me questions that helped me to revise. Sometimes, she would say, "what I think
you mean to say is. . . ." I would quickly scribble her words, later lifting
them entirely as I typed a final draft. How did she know what I meant
to say? How did she know what questions to ask? Why didn't I think to
ask these questions? At the time, I believed this friend was smarter than
I was; I thought maybe she had worked harder in high school. I believed this in spite of the relaxed attitude she took toward school, in
spite of the fact that late into the evening while I was typing my drafts,

she was making popcorn and chatting with friends, joking about her habits of procrastination.

It was this same friend who once took me aside to point out a grammatical error that I made regularly in conversation. "The correct form," she said, "is 'My paper needs to be revised' or 'My paper needs revising.' You always say," she smiled kindly, "'My paper needs revised.' I thought since you're an English major that you would want to know that was not grammatically correct." I appreciated her comments, but I wondered if other expressions I had learned in my Pittsburgh working-class neighborhood were marking me as different. To this day, "needs revised," "needs washed," "needs cleaned," "needs tutored" still sound right to me. In conversation, I have to anticipate the construction and mentally reconfigure the way I would naturally say it. Thirty years later, after having lived in middle-class circumstances in the Midwest, there are still times when I slip back into old patterns. Old voices sneak back across the border when I am distracted, ad-libbing, or arguing, times when my mental border guard forgets to pay attention.

My "writing tutor" in college was like many middle-class students whose parents are college-educated professionals and who attended well-funded suburban schools. They seem to just naturally do better in school. They have been prepped for school success since they were infants, absorbing the cultural habits of the school system through their skin. When students like these use writing centers, they often benefit from a few questions or suggestions that remind them of what they already know. But students whose families live outside this preferred social structure often find school less familiar. Too often they blame themselves for not having what it takes to succeed, or too readily they reject the school culture, defining themselves in opposition to it. As a college student, I attributed my friend's skillful performances to individual talent and my struggles to lack of talent. No doubt our individual talents varied, but there were also significant unacknowledged differences in our class backgrounds. My friend knew, for example, how to conduct herself at the social gathering our history professor held at his home because she had witnessed such gatherings at her parents' home. I stuck close to her side that night because I was unsure of what people talked about at such events. I attributed my behavior to shyness. I wasn't able to see that my cultural experience had taught me how to conduct a conversation with neighbors who joined the family for a beer on the front porch during a summer evening but not how to circulate at a gathering where people stood around drinking martinis. I thought the problem I had with writing and with social interaction was located in my personality or in my brain rather than in the lack of a particular kind of cultural experience. I did what my friend told me to do and said what she told me to say because I could not imagine options that allowed for more negotiation.

Writing center people often catch glimpses of the gaps between academic expectations and students' cultural experiences, but generally they believe that students need to learn academic literacy because . . . well, because if they don't . . . it will hurt them in the long run . . . because that's the way things work . . . in the real world. The string of indeterminate "becauses" protects us from questioning our actions and limits how deeply we look at the way academic expectations regulate student performances. The common assumption is that the more a student thinks, talks, writes, reads, and values like the dominant culture, the more rewards he or she will reap. So the "right" thing to do is to prepare students for the way that world operates. If an advanced level of literacy guarantees access to professional positions, then tutoring literacy must be a naturally helpful activity, innocent of implication in politics or ideology. At least it appears innocent until we enter into the perspectives of students who come from cultures that are not congruent with the mainstream culture of the school. Nagging questions form in the back of our minds when we encounter students like Joe, Patty, and Mary. In our work with students like these, we begin to see how the tacit expectations of schools, assignments, and evaluation systems make it difficult for some students to "earn" the good grades that come more readily to students from the dominant culture. Because it is difficult to find language to articulate the troubling contradictions that literacy learning creates for these students, writing center work is depicted in innocent ways—as "helping" students in the unfriendly world of academia—even though we are merely helping them conform to institutional expectations.

My argument in this chapter is deceptively simple: I believe writing centers can do a better job of supporting students if we stop locating literacy problems in individuals and instead locate them in cultural constructions. But the dimensions of this argument are complex. To locate literacy problems in cultural constructions, we must abandon positions of innocence guaranteed by the literacy myth and come to terms with the political implications of writing center work. We must also pay a great deal more attention to the cultural assumptions that we bring to writing center work. My aim in this chapter is not to dim the enthusiasm of writing center workers but rather to draw attention to the historical and cultural context that informs our work, to expose the social tensions that have always lurked under the surface of literacy work, and to theorize ways of engaging those tensions. I believe that the rapid cultural changes of postmodernity create opportunities for writing centers to negotiate more socially just literacy practices, but to do so writing center workers need a stronger sense of their historical positioning as literacy agents. To accomplish this, I provide an argument that conceptualizes literacy as ideological work rather than a neutral skill. To strengthen this argument, I show how naturalized assumptions embedded in mainstream literacy practices undermine individual efforts and reproduce social divisions. Finally, I propose ways of engaging critically with commonsense notions of literacy as well as ways to reconceptualize literacy for postmodern times. I hope to provide enough evidence in this chapter to reconstruct the writing center's relationship with literacy. If student writers can understand that cultural constructions of meaning exist outside themselves, they can choose not to accept positions that undermine their individual histories and motivations.

Literacy as Ideological Work Rather Than Neutral Skill

Literacy researcher Brian Street, drawing on his own study of Maktab literacy in Iran as well as his review of literacy research around the world, offers a way of conceptualizing literacy that calls attention to the ideological and cultural values carried in literacy practices. He contrasts two models of literacy: the autonomous model and the ideological model. The autonomous model presents the dominant standard of literacy as a culturally neutral, individually acquired, and context-free skill. Until recently, the autonomous model has prevailed in Western schooling, anthropological research, and economic development. Using evidence from anthropologists and historians who have studied literacy, Street shows that claims for the neutrality and objectivity of literacy skills are self-interested and ethnocentric. The autonomous model insists that the dominant literacy is neutral, but it also uses markers of this literacy for political purposes, ranking and sorting people based on features of their texts. Street terms this a "sleight of hand." He calls attention to the way that adherents of the autonomous model emphasize the neutrality and value-free nature of their own literacy conventions but still "attempt to maintain that their own conventions are superior" (1984, 29). Much of the political power of dominant literacy is located in the indirect and tacit nature of this move.

In the autonomous model, writing center work appears innocent and helpful. Writing centers are supposed to support nonmainstream students so that they can learn the skills necessary to be successful in an educational system that wasn't designed with them in mind. When literacy is understood as a neutral skill detached from culture, the literacy practices of school seem to be universal, the way that good people naturally behave. As literacy theorist James Gee writes, "Each Discourse protects itself by demanding from its adherents performances which act as though its ways of being, thinking, acting, talking, writing, reading, and valuing are right, natural, obvious, the way good and intelligent and normal people behave" (1996, 190–91). If one believes that a particular form of discourse is "right" or "natural" or "better," the obvious conclusion is that those who depart from this form are "wrong" and that they need help to learn the "correct" way to do things. If the literacy of the dominant class is "naturally" better, then writing center workers do not need to think about what positions them to help others. Their innocence is guaranteed by the discursive formation that structures school.

However, many modernist assumptions about individual autonomy get in the way of providing authentic support to the students who come to writing centers. The collaborative talk of the writing center always has to be carefully qualified so that it doesn't appear that writing center tutors are telling students what to think. Writing center tutors are often trained to take a "hands-off" approach so that they do not appear to be doing the work for students, undermining individual autonomy and responsibility. Writing center tutors are supposed to use a nondirective pedagogy to help students "discover" what they want to say. These approaches protect the status quo and withhold insider knowledge, inadvertently keeping students from nonmainstream cultures on the sidelines, making them guess about what the mainstream culture expects or frustrating them into less productive attitudes. These approaches enact the belief that what is expected is natural behavior rather than culturally specific performance.

Street contrasts the autonomous model of literacy with an ideological model. The ideological model acknowledges that literacies are embedded in social practices that carry cultural values. The ideological model of literacy recognizes that literacy has political significance, that the teaching of literacy is caught up in stratified social structures, and that forms of literacy, such as oral and written modes, cannot be isolated and taught as neutral and separate skills. From an ideological perspective, we can see that academic literacy recruits us into a particular ideology, calling us to assent to a system that privileges some people more than others. If we take an ideological perspective on this process rather than innocently consent to business as usual, we imagine alternative practices by shifting our focus from the individual who is constructed as lacking skills to the system that structures what we do.

Let me illustrate the differences between the two models by returning to the example of Mary. From an autonomous perspective, when Mary arrives at writing center walk-in hours with a draft that demonstrates conservative religious beliefs, she as a *person* poses a problem to her writing center tutor. If her tutor believes that learning to question received wisdom and to read all texts critically is a necessary and naturally superior skill in literacy learning, then Mary, who appears to uncritically accept the wisdom of elders and who holds some texts holy, appears to be wrong, naive, or at best unenlightened. Within this scenario, negotiating between Mary's religious tradition and the academic tradition is very delicate business, an interaction that would make many tutors uneasy. A tutor might suggest that Mary should perhaps reconsider the readings in her course anthology, hoping that as she rereads these essays she will come to see the limits of her traditional ways.

If instead Mary's literacy is considered within an ideological framework, a tutor might see that Mary comes to walk-in hours to "get her grammar checked" because she knows that something cultural is at stake in her writing, and "grammar" is a word she has for trying to understand it. The focus can shift from the individual (Mary) to the cultural work of literacy. A tutor might then talk with Mary about how the *assignment* constructs her as a media-literate, urban, religiously uncommitted liberal person, all of which she is not. This approach shifts attention away from Mary and onto an artifact of academic literacy—the assignment sheet. With this shift, Mary and her tutor can talk about the options for engaging with the way the assignment constructs her and speculate about the consequences of resisting, negotiating, or accommodating the tacit cultural expectations of the assignment. If Mary wants to write a paper that resists the construction of the assignment, a tutor can propose strategies. For example, to convince the teacher that she understands the construction of the assignment, Mary can begin her paper by calling attention to the kind of student invoked by the assignment and announce her intention to write from an alternate subjectivity. The focus of the writing center session would *not* be on what is lacking in Mary but on how she is being constructed by an academic literacy practice and how she wants to negotiate with that construction.

Within an ideological model of literacy, writing center people would deliberately call attention to the ways that literacy practices carry cultural knowledge, ideology, and values. Academic literacy would not be imagined as an individual skill but instead as a set of cultural practices. Writing center workers would talk about the beliefs encoded in these practices, making the tacit understandings explicit, offering students more choices and more information about how these practices work. Within an ideological understanding of literacy, rather than ignore cultural variables—gender, race, age, class, ethnicity, sexual orientation, institutional status—that often visibly mark our positioning in institutions, we would call attention to the ways that these variables both shape and limit our perspectives, acknowledging that the map we use to understand that system is influenced by our particular history in the institution.

Once we acknowledge that literacy practices are cultural rather than natural, we need to be much more aware of how culture works, making explicit that which we take for granted and articulating that which has always seemed "natural." Such conscious practice is difficult for a number of reasons. For one, culture is learned through assimilation rather than direct teaching. We absorb it as children; therefore, transmitting cultural understanding as adults is difficult. Usually we are unaware of what is "cultural" about our "normal" ways of interacting with language until we experience cultural conflict. Another reason this is difficult is that if we are members of the culture of power—the dominant white middle class—we are unaccustomed to having our way of doing things challenged, and we have little if any experience understanding ourselves as members of a "culture." The literacy myth has naturalized the dominant ideology carried in the literacy practices of school to the extent that mainstream teachers and tutors are rarely even aware when their expectations are causing conflict or confusion for students. Also, as long as teachers and tutors are sure that they are already doing the "right" thing, they are unlikely to change; who willingly wants to trade innocence for implication in unjust practices? Instead, when students perform in ways that are difficult for academics to understand, their performances are negatively evaluated; differences in literacies are presumed wrong.

Not only does the dominant culture confuse what is cultural with what is normal, but as Lisa Delpit argues, members of the culture of power often operate "under the assumption that to make any rules or expectations explicit is to act against liberal principles, to limit the freedom and autonomy of those subjected to the implicitness" (1995, 26). The friend who acted as my writing tutor in the dorm violated some of these liberal principles by directly telling me what I meant to say and by deliberately calling attention to my spoken grammatical errors, contrasting the way that I spoke with the correct way of speaking. I violated the liberal code of ethics by lifting her words into my papers. The writing center codes about not telling students what to say, not putting words into their mouths, not telling them how to organize their papers, not undermining teachers' authority, and not proofreading student papers, all need to be rethought if we practice an ideological understanding of academic literacy.

Rethinking these codes is not a simple matter of repudiating them but instead developing a more fine-grained understanding of how one acquires a literacy that is not "natural." For students who are not already members of the dominant group, the process has to be denaturalized and made much more explicit. Writing center work may initially need to be more time-intensive, both for the writing tutor who needs time to figure out how to explain what he or she has always taken for granted and for the student who needs more time to practice

doing what does not come "naturally." If it has been natural for someone to say, "this paper needs revised" for eighteen years, it may well
take a few years to denaturalize this speech pattern. Writing center
policies about how much time is appropriate to allocate to any one student are often driven by assumptions that do not take into account how
long literacy acquisition takes. Writing center tutors can also be much
more *direct* about academic expectations without being *directive*. College
students from cultures outside the dominant middle class are not immature or undeveloped users of language in their own culture. When
writing center workers learn to address cultural expectations directly
and explicitly so that students can understand the values at stake in
competing frameworks, students can make more informed decisions
about how they want to perform.

Literacy Teaching Replicates
the Social Structure

Naturalized assumptions about the neutrality of dominant literacy are
pervasive; they extend far beyond school settings and are used in tacit
ways to construct relationships of power and authority. Because autonomous literacy is deeply embedded in the structure of school as well
as other social structures, these naturalized expectations influence institutional relationships. Literacy is linked to the myth of meritocracy,
the belief that the American public education system guarantees equal
opportunity to all individuals who work hard, so we easily "forget" that
literacy learning is not always a happy march of individual progress but
really a matter of conforming to predetermined expectations.

Ellen Barton's research shows how naturalized expectations about
literacy structure relationships even in medical settings. Barton's analysis of the interactions between Medicaid families and medical professionals shows that class-based assumptions about literacy often create
"adversarial rather than collaborative relationships" (1997, 420). Interactions that were intended to provide care often turned into interactions where literacy was used to threaten and to interrogate rather than
to communicate because of naturalized assumptions about how "compliant" families should behave. Unspoken middle-class expectations
about who controls the conversation, about what level of detail is appropriate, and about who is responsible for record keeping influenced
the way authority and power were used in the interactions. Even
though the medical professionals in her study provided high-quality
care, they made quick judgments about working-class families' marital
status, living arrangements, and ability to follow recommendations,
and they often failed to provide the logistical support that compliance

with medical recommendations often requires. Barton contrasts the negative interactions of Medicaid families with those of highly educated families, who demonstrated compliant literacy behaviors (bringing "exemplary" written records in "pseudo-medical style") in order to achieve collaborative relationships with medical professionals.

To illustrate the ideological power of these naturalized assumptions and their effect on individual lives, I share a story about another writing center student, Rebecca.[1] As I write this chapter, Rebecca is completing her final year at the university. She has worked in our writing center since her first term in college, initially as a student with a weekly appointment, then as an office assistant in a work-study program and now as a writing coach. I will use Rebecca's own words, taken from tape-recorded meetings, to show the ways her literacy education interacted with her personal and economic history to isolate her, to erode her self-esteem, and to leave her unaware of opportunities. Raised by a single mother in a small rural town, the second-born of three children, Rebecca experienced the stigma of living in the small town's government-subsidized apartments. As she explains it, "As soon as my first boyfriend found out where I lived, he broke up with me. It took me almost two years to bring the next boyfriend to my house, and I was very scared when I did."

Rebecca's early placement in a low reading group replicated the social structure of the small town:

> I remember being in the low reading group. I don't know if that made a difference, but the kids in the low reading group weren't popular. I was always really good at math. But because [the teachers and the middle-class students] associated me with the low reading group, they thought I wasn't good in all my subjects. Most of the kids in the low reading group didn't go to college. And in middle school, they were considered still at that low rank. I agree that I needed more help, but I disagree with the program taught. The teacher tried hard to cover up the differences between the different groups. No matter how hard the teachers tried, the children always knew and because of this I shied away from reading. The result of this is that I still have a very hard time pronouncing words and writing papers. I also have a very poor vocabulary.

Rebecca demonstrates awareness of what influenced her teachers' assumptions about her ability and interest. Of her experience in elementary school, she comments:

> In a small town they [the teachers] know who you are and where you live. And I didn't live in the good part; I lived in low-income apartments. And they knew that. They knew I didn't have money. In classes, say you had to get picked to do fun stuff, like go to other things, they

> always picked the upper [class] kids. They never picked me. Unless I
> went up there and said, "Well, I want to do it."

When Rebecca started college, she found the experience of living in
residence halls where "everyone has the same things" liberating. But
she soon discovered that the early stigma stayed with her. She described a visit to a college friend's family:

> I actually thought I was getting over it until I went downstate with my
> friends, and I realized how scared I was. I couldn't get myself to talk
> with them [my friend's family]. I just felt so nervous when I got there.
> I thought people were looking at me and thinking "Oh, no, she's not
> our type." I worry about the way I dress. I think it comes from being
> poor when I was little. I take it very to heart when they say I talk like
> a Yooper. I take it to heart. It will stay in my head the rest of the day.

Rebecca's relationship with authority figures, her motivation to do well
in school, her persistent financial challenges, and her self-consciousness
about her personal history all interact in complex and sometimes contradictory ways to impact her performance at the university. On the
surface, Rebecca is the kind of student a teacher might say is not working up to her ability, perhaps not applying herself strategically or perhaps letting herself get too distracted by college social issues.

Commenting on her first experience with college composition,
Rebecca relates how hard she worked, how many people had read her
papers, how frustrated she was when her teacher gave her a final grade
of C+ and told her that "something was missing" in her papers. She had
used our writing center regularly during that term but sometimes overlooked her writing coach's suggestions for revision because she had
been taught to pay more attention to surface features rather than the
deeper structure of her essays. She was the type of student that writing
center workers and teachers tell to work harder, to get an earlier start
on their papers, to improve their attendance records, to follow directions. Because of our naturalized assumptions, we might think that students like Rebecca are resistant to suggestion or else unwilling to work
hard enough to succeed. Rarely are we aware of the social conflict occurring beneath the surface of what looks like "C+" work. When, like
the medical professionals, we locate the problem in students' lack of
compliance, we protect ourselves from the challenge of articulating
what is missing in their papers. In this way, we preserve the "culture of
power" (Delpit 1988).

Some might suggest that "individualized instruction" is the best
thing for Rebecca, that we need to identify her deficiencies, explain the
middle-class cultural values that she is "missing," provide her with the
knowledge that middle-class kids gain when they are growing up. But
to show students like Rebecca how to earn more than a C+, we would

need to unpack the tacit expectations about how to use literacy to acknowledge expertise, how to show respect for authority, how to play the academic game of "earning" a collaborative rather than an adversarial relationship with a teacher or writing coach. We might even talk about other things like how to set a table for company dinner, how to get your pronouns and verbs to match, how to make a salad with more than iceberg lettuce, how to critique TV and movies, how to chat during cocktail hour.

But that's not how we usually think of individualized instruction. We claim we don't tell students what to do nor do we tell them what they should know. Instead, we explain that tutors encourage independence, assist with the acquisition of strategic knowledge, provide supportive listening for affective concerns like writing anxiety, and interpret the meaning of academic language (see, for example, Muriel Harris' "Talking in the Middle" [1995]). Sure, Rebecca benefits from these things—but she wants more than a C+. Can we tell her also what is missing in her papers? Not if we are practicing nondirective tutoring, not if we believe the problem lies in Rebecca rather than in tacit cultural expectations carried in literacy practices, and not if our institutional practices have already convinced Rebecca that the problem lies within her. I think it is more ethical to unpack these values and assumptions than to pretend that they don't exist, to juxtapose, for example, the working-class cultural values carried in neighborhood and family literacy practices with the middle-class cultural values carried in academic literacy practices and to explain their arbitrariness as well as the inevitable use of middle-class practices to label and exclude.

As I talked with Rebecca, I slowly began to realize the extent to which our own writing center practices replicated the status quo. During her second and third year at the university, the financial aid office placed Rebecca in a work-study position in our writing center. Welcoming her as an office helper, we gave her the routine chores of filing, watering plants, and photocopying, all of which she performed as she listened to the nice middle-class undergraduate writing coaches engaged in an entirely different kind of activity. Theoretically, we knew that one doesn't learn a community's language habits and values by sitting on the sidelines looking in. In fact, the sidelined position guarantees that the excluded person's language will remain the same because language learning occurs through a process of participation rather than observation. As we learned to question the status quo, we invited Rebecca to apply to be a writing coach, but first we had to convince her that we thought she could do it. In that position, she has exceeded her own expectations as well as ours. Because of her lived experience, Rebecca has a better sense of what is helpful than do those of us who have rarely needed help with literacy. Because of her lived experience,

Rebecca's intuition about what a student doesn't understand is finely tuned. Students value her natural directness and her to-the-point suggestions. Later, we invited Rebecca to join us in writing a conference paper; and again she exceeded expectations, refocusing us with straightforward questions as we drafted our papers and displaying more perspective than I could muster when repeated scheduling changes interfered with our plans. Rebecca has convinced me that cultural expectations are where the problem lies. But learning to think outside of naturalized expectations is especially difficult because cultural common sense works against it. In the next section, I provide some of the historical evidence that challenges common sense.

Complicating Cultural Common Sense with History

It is far easier to trust an institution than to trust an individual without power, easier to blame students like Rebecca than to scrutinize school practices. To work against the tendency to hold institutions innocent, we must develop ways of thinking critically and historically about the work of literacy. The enlightenment dream, which has structured our institutions for a long time, rests on the assumption that we can achieve a better world if we all learn to communicate rationally in a transparently clear, culturally neutral, coherent language. Modernity, with its belief in reason, progress, and development, sutures autonomous literacy with the cultural narrative of progress that is inextricably linked with the American belief in meritocracy and individualism. Writing centers exist on many campuses to support the enlightenment dream, and writing center workers are surrounded by expectations that they should help students understand what's wrong with the way they use literacy in order to ensure the dream.

　　These beliefs—in culturally neutral language, in progress, in individual achievement, in literacy, and in schooling—have become so interwoven and widespread that they have formed a narrative and have achieved the status of myth. The literacy myth is a peculiarly sanitized and popularized symbolic narrative, drained of the rich paradoxes found in traditional myths. As such, it serves a protective function, covering social tensions with a warm blanket of common sense. The literacy myth has naturalized our social structure, "rendering any alternative to it unthinkable" (Eagleton 1991, 188). Eagleton reminds us that "myth is not just any old falsehood: we would not describe as a myth the claim that Everest can be scaled in forty minutes at a brisk trot" (188). To qualify as mythical, Eagleton explains, a belief has "to be widely shared and reflect some significant psychological investment on the part of its adherents" (189). Myth, Roland Barthes explains, serves a harmonizing function. It explains the world not as it is, but as it wants to be. To expose a myth is to cut oneself off from the many "who are entertained or warmed" by myth (1972, 156–57).

The literacy myth teaches us to think of literacy as an unequivocally good thing, something that improves a person's position in life. The achievement of advanced literacy is supposed to make us better people, better citizens, and better workers, especially in the information age when so much work depends on the ability to manage information. When literacy is conceptualized only in positive, mythical terms, we lose sight of its paradoxical effects. When I was a child, my mother often urged me "get your nose out of books for a while" because she wanted her daughter to participate in the real life around her, not just the manufactured life on the pages of books. On an intuitive level my mother understood the paradox of literacy: it both connects and separates, liberates and controls, empowers and limits. While books may extend a child's horizons, they simultaneously limit her interactions with daily life.

To place writing center work more fully in the paradox of literacy, it is useful to understand the complicated political function of the literacy myth. After an extensive study of the uses of literacy in the Western world, literacy historian Harvey Graff (1991a, 1991b) concluded that the literacy myth is a tool of hegemony, the political process whereby the dominant group secures consent for its practices by virtue of its social and intellectual prestige and its superior economic position. According to Graff, the literacy myth works as a hegemonic (and therefore political) tool because it calls us to assent to a meaning system that appears innocent and is sanctioned by our social institutions. Through the work of our institutions—churches, schools, hospitals—we become accustomed to accepting the views of the dominant class. In school we learn that speaking and writing Standard English is a sign of intelligence, so as adults we are confident we are doing "the right thing" when we deny those who speak a nonmainstream or "nonstandard" discourse the jobs or the good grades or the promotions we give to those who speak standard discourse. In college classrooms and writing centers, the writing of American minority students who are bidialectical or bilingual is described as incoherent and nonstandard because it doesn't conform to mainstream worldviews and language patterns. Mainstream rhetorical strategies are imagined as culturally neutral.

Because hegemony is not a coercive political process, its direction can be changed; however, changing a hegemonic direction is made difficult by the absence of language to define an alternative interpretation of reality. As Victor Villanueva Jr. puts it, "There is discomfort, but not language with which to explain the discomfort" (1993, 124). In the writing center, we might observe the conflicts of students like Joe, who earns his A by silencing his experience in order to write a paper that conforms to expectations, but we "forget" those conflicts if we accept the literacy myth, believing that conventional literacy learning is always "for their own good." We lack the theoretical language for explaining that Joe has encountered a cultural conflict created by the assumption that an assignment asking students to write from sources found in the library is ideologically neutral.

Hegemonic beliefs sustain cultural systems not because we are all dupes and believe whatever our culture teaches us but because these beliefs offer explanations for issues that cannot otherwise be comfortably explained. Americans are uncomfortable with the persistence of class, race, and ethnic discrimination, so we use literacy to explain it away: working-class people earn less because they speak a nonstandard English, or working-class students get lower grades because their writing is undeveloped. Through the process of hegemony, mainstream literacy becomes associated with individual achievement, rational thought, moral and ethical behavior, employment opportunities, greater capacity for empathy, and increased democratic participation. People whose literacy is not mainstream are perceived as less deserving of social power and social rewards. Signs of illiteracy are associated with irrational behavior, laziness, unemployment, criminality, and medical emergencies caused by caregivers who cannot read directions on an aspirin bottle. Because the literacy myth organizes our thinking and our institutions, we "forget" that literacy (including standards of correctness and adequate development) is culturally specific; we forget that literacy is used to separate and rank people; we forget that we need more than one kind of literacy to interact effectively in a diverse world.

Because of the strongly individualistic nature of American culture, during times of rapid social change we tend to blame individuals for not keeping up rather than locate tensions in changing conditions. John Trimbur observes that during times of intense change, "fear about downward mobility and loss of status has repeatedly been displaced and refigured as a fear of the alien and the other—whether Irish Catholics in the 1840s, southern and eastern Europeans in the 1890s, or Hispanics and Asians in the 1980s" (1991, 293). Similarly, literacy historian Harvey J. Graff observes that something "much more than literacy levels or test results [was] at stake" during the so-called literacy crisis of the late twentieth century (1991a, 390). He characterizes the mid-to-late 1970s and early 1980s as a time of intense national concern about "international status, power, productivity, well-being, inflation, security, energy supplies, and confidence in leadership and institutions" (391).

Interestingly, the late 1970s and early 1980s were the years when many writing centers were first established. During this time, the dramatic shifts in the economy and the resulting changes in the population of students seeking college degrees were not usually factored in to explain the discrepancies between the literacies the new students brought to college and the literacy the professors expected them to have. Instead, students were perceived as "having problems" indicating a lack of aptitude, application, and motivation. After all, English was taught in all twelve grades. If "correct" usage hadn't been mastered in that amount of time, how could these new students be considered "college material"? In archival materials at Michigan Tech, I found a memo written in 1974 by the first director of our writing center. He announced the opening of what was then called the Language Skills Lab using a parody of the poetic inscription on the Statue of Liberty

> Send us your tiresome, your non-passes,
> Your befuddled toots yearning to write "real fab."
> The wretched writers of your teeming classes.
> Send these, the comma faulters, syntax-tost to writing lab.

Rather than address the ways the automobile industry was changing, resulting in the loss of blue-collar jobs in Michigan, the professor focuses on the students, describing them as "tiresome," "befuddled," and "wretched." When this professor hired me to be a tutor in 1978, he warned me not to spend too much time with any one student because "most of them probably won't make it anyway." His behavior may strike many readers as callous and elitist, but he was really a kind man and had given considerable attention to designing the new lab. I doubt if he was aware of the cultural script he was enacting and the way the literacy myth functioned to locate the problem of changing social and economic conditions in students.

There is plenty of historical and anthropological evidence that literacy has been used repeatedly to "manage" social change rather than attend to individuals' best interests. According to literacy researcher Jenny Cook-Gumperz, schooled literacy in the eighteenth century grew out of the dominant class' desire to maintain a pool of manual labor. Prior to the eighteenth century, the conception of literacy was pluralistic: a variety of reading and writing skills and a multiplicity of literacies were recognized as having both social and recreational value. The dominant group feared that this popular literacy would diminish the pool of manual labor and lead to social unrest, so school systems were designed to bring this popular literacy under control. This "changed forever the relationship of the majority of the population to their own talents for learning and for literacy" (1986, 26–27). The earlier acceptance of pluralistic literacy did not lend itself to separation or ranking, but the new schooled literacy led to standardization, stratification, and systemization, a handy function in a growing capitalistic society (30).

Schooled literacy was designed to normalize, to manage difference; it has a history of separating people from their own desires to know and to communicate.

Another example of the use of literacy to manage social change can be found in Janet Duitsman Cornelius' study of literacy and slavery in the antebellum South. Cornelius notes that prior to the Civil War, slave literacy was carefully monitored and controlled by slave owners and state legislatures. A few Southerners argued that literacy, particularly the ability to read the Bible, would encourage slaves to be more obedient and compliant; other voices feared that "if slaves learned to read the Bible, they'd realize how short their owners fell of their Christian duty" (1992, 138–39). Slaves who found ways of their own to learn to read and write were severely punished—they were branded, they were sold without their families, they were whipped, their fingers were amputated. After the Civil War, the literacy level of African Americans rose from 7 percent at the time of emancipation to more than 90 percent in 1950. Contrary to cultural common sense, this rise in levels of literacy did not combat racism. Graff observes from his studies that "as levels of literacy among blacks rose, race became more important, and literacy less so, in determining occupational levels" (1991a, 363). In fact, contrary to the popular belief that high levels of literacy are a sign of an advanced civilization, Graff's extensive study of the history of literacy in Western culture led him to conclude: "Contrary to popular and scholarly wisdom, major steps forward in trade, commerce, and even industry took place in some periods and places with remarkably low levels of literacy; conversely, higher levels of literacy have not proved to be stimulants for 'modern' economic developments" (10–11). Nor did Graff find evidence that advanced levels of literacy led to individual achievement. In fact, Graff's evidence suggests that ethnicity and social class were much stronger predictors of educational and economic achievement. Like Cook-Gumperz, Graff observes that literacy "contributed regularly as an element of the structure of inequality, reinforcing the steep ridges of stratification." Although literacy did not universally benefit those who had attained it, "neither did it disadvantage all those who had not" (1991b, 19).

In addition to historical evidence of the (mis)use of literacy to manage or monitor social change, we also have evidence from literacy anthropologists that contradicts the common claim that achieving literacy expands and deepens the capacity for critical thought. For example, Sylvia Scribner and Michael Cole's (1988) study of Vai literacy in northwestern Liberia, a literacy learned in nonschool settings, led them to comment on the "frailty" of claims for the cognitive consequences of literacy. They noted that schooling and urban experience had more influence on cognitive skills than did literacy. They also found that cognitive skills were often domain specific and not transferable to other settings. Extensive research literature documents that the ability to transfer cognitive understanding from one domain to another is "routinely missing" (Gardner 1991, 5–6). Scribner and Cole's research also calls attention to the impact of cultural values and social relationships on literacy learning, noting that Vai literacy is usually learned within a short time frame (two weeks to two months) and without specialized teaching materials. Scribner and Cole connect the speed of the learning with the ways in which Vai literacy is sustained by personal and cultural values, noting how rarely Western institutional literacy taps into indigenous interests. Mary Louise Pratt (1991) makes a similar observation when she observes how her young son's interest in baseball cards led him into an integrated learning experience that was far more meaningful than anything his schooling offered him. Another anthropologist, Frederick Erickson (1988), also addresses this issue. He raises the question of why children as young as one or two years can master a spoken language, a task far more cognitively complex than learning to read, yet many of the same children cannot learn to read in school. He concludes that an individual's ability is arbitrarily defined by his social relationship with the people in the institution.

How can writing centers come to terms with all this historical and anthropological evidence that literacy often functions to disguise other social and political interests? What can writing centers do when they are surrounded by commonsense assumptions about literacy? We cannot deny that communicative competence is necessary for academic and professional success. There is truth as well as psychological investment in cultural common sense. Our colleagues, relatives, and friends who bring their concerns about literacy to us want assurance that someone is doing something about "the problem." Rather than react to cultural common sense with annoyance (which on my worse days I certainly feel) or deny its truth function, I need to find ways to extend and complicate it. Cultural common sense is fragmentary and contradictory. Encounters with commonsense notions of literacy provide us with opportunities to historicize and elaborate it, exposing its contradictions, "renovating and making critical" (Gramsci 1971, 331) existing beliefs. Gee suggests a similar strategy. He concluded from his own efforts to study literacy that "the clearest way to see the workings of language and literacy was to displace literacy from the center of attention, moving society, culture, and values to the foreground" (1996, vii). Whether concerns about literacy are expressed by colleagues or by relatives, the expression itself is an opportunity to shift the focus away from the individuals in question to the economic and social transformations of the time period. Just recently, a colleague complained to me about students' lack of cultural literacy, sharing the story of how one of his students had to ask what kind of punishment was meant by "capital punishment." Rather than reinforce his fears about what students don't know, I can instead comment on the realities of living in the information age where none of us feel we know enough about all we should know; I can talk about how much more students know today about science, mathematics, and technology than I do, and I can compliment him on having established an environment in which students are unafraid to ask basic questions.

In my encounters with family members who inevitably engage me in conversations about their perceptions of the decline of literacy, I have opportunities to remind them of our shared educational histories. As the grandchildren of immigrants, we attended schools in working-class neighborhoods where our English teachers focused on eliminating traces of ethnic accents, ungrammatical expressions, and idiosyncratic penmanship. They taught us to use language "correctly" rather than use it differently or use it with pleasure. I can complicate common sense if I remind them that all of us learned at some point that learning to be correct and neat was not all there was to being literate. I can also point out, as do literacy historians Lauren Resnick and Daniel Resnick (1977), that at this point in history we demand a much higher degree of literacy from a much greater portion of the population than we ever have before, and I can compare these changed expectations to others that are more familiar. Uncle Walter's career as a choir director, for example, spanned both pre- and post-Vatican II. As a result of the changes in the Catholic Church required by Vatican II, he had to work through the transition from a liturgy focused solely on the performance of a single priest and an all-male choir to a liturgy that drew parishioners into participation. When Uncle Walter complains about the decline of literacy, I can remind him how difficult it continues to be to draw traditionally silent members into participation. Uncle Walter needed not only to find music that was attractive and suitable to a wider range of voices, but also to train his ears to hear more voices—some inevitably discordant—and to teach himself to experience pleasure in getting more people to sing.

In my efforts to complicate common sense, I can also point to ways that we tend to pathologize literacy problems. As a second grader, my brother was placed in a school for the blind, hearing impaired, and deaf because his teachers were not able to teach him to read. As a child, he was traumatized by that experience, and his stay at that school ended after a year. He is now president of one of the country's largest retail firms. His success in the fiercely competitive retail business is due to literacies that were not valued in school. He knows how to position himself favorably in a variety of contexts; he operates from a natural curiosity about how things work; he insists on answers to his own questions. His success illustrates the inadequacy of an educational agenda of assimilation that overemphasizes correctness. Besides, if the literacy myth's claim that greater literacy leads to economic success were completely true, then I, the big sister who "always had her nose in a book" would be making more money.

When my cousin, a university professor and therapist, complains that her students are "fundamentally illiterate," I can respond with an invitation to help me figure out how our education taught us to make judgments about a person's character and chances for success based on language use. When my brother-in-law bemoans that his new hires, all college graduates, "can't write," I can comment that writing well in the workplace is predicated on understanding the performances that are expected and the values, moves, and thought patterns that are rewarded in that firm. Writing well in composition class will not ensure the ability to write well in a new neighborhood, a new career, or a new discipline because literacy practices are context dependent.

Rather than respond to my colleagues' or relatives' commonsense notions of literacy with yet another effort to explain the complex nature of the writing process or the diverse range of ways our writing center supports students, I can instead elaborate and historicize their commonsense understandings of literacy. The frequent comments about literacy that emerge in conversations with relatives and colleagues indicate their desire to position themselves amidst the change. If writing center workers respond in ways that focus attention on the rapid cultural changes under way rather than on unskilled or undeveloped individuals, we provide a map for repositioning. Because literacy is not culturally neutral, even though many pretend it is, changes in literacy involve changes in our understandings of identity, politics, and relationships. Recognizing the commonsense truth value in the literacy myth—the fact that when literacy changes, so does everything else—will do more to productively situate the social fears circulating around literacy than will responding in ways that confirm literacy as a neutral, culturally independent, autonomous individual skill.

Resnick and Resnick argue that literacy crises are manufactured whenever the culture raises its expectations of what counts as literacy and extends it to a larger population but does not change its forms of pedagogy (1977, 202). Deborah Brandt explains that when cultural expectations of literacy change, the older expectations remain, accumulating at the site of new expectations and causing cultural confusion and dismay. Recently, for example, concern was raised about a reported decline in penmanship. While we now expect students to meet a higher literacy standard than ever before—the ability to critically read unfamiliar texts, respond coherently to unfamiliar prompts, and demonstrate facility with word-processing systems—we still expect high-quality penmanship, particularly from those with less social power. As Brandt explains, not only do materials and practices from earlier times linger at the site of new expectations, but connotations that cling to literacy— moral, religious, mannerly, elite—pile up and "haunt the sites of literacy learning" (1995, 665). Brandt argues that the surplus of meanings calls for new approaches to literacy learning, ones that involve detecting the "residual, emergent, often conflicted contexts of literacy" and assisting students as they "position and reposition" themselves amidst the changing forms (666). I believe that when writing centers talk with students about how literacy works as a cultural practice, we do more for them than when we pretend that it is a neutral individual skill. If we explain the cultural values, beliefs, and performance expectations that are encoded in academic practices, if we make the tacit understandings explicit, we are creating more choices and offering students more information about how culture works. However, in exchange for cutting ourselves off from the "many who are entertained or warmed" by the innocence connected with the literacy myth, writing center people will need to articulate a vision of literacy for postmodern times. If writing center workers get in the habit of critiquing and historicising commonsense notions of literacy but are unable to offer alternative conceptions of literacy, they won't be popular with either students or teachers. Coming to terms with a loss of innocence should not mean becoming cynical. Because commonsense notions of literacy are culturally powerful and ubiquitous, writing center workers must be prepared to offer more compelling and more socially just visions of literacy to counteract the simplistic understandings that lend themselves to social ranking rather than communication.

What, Then, Counts as Literacy?

Brandt speculates that literate ability at the end of the century "may be best measured as a person's capacity to amalgamate new reading and writing practices in response to rapid social change" (1995, 651). In postmodern times, writing center workers must be able to (1) recognize the type of literacy called for in a particular context; (2) translate that expectation to students who may have a different sense of what counts as literacy; and (3) map the conflicting expectations for students so they become adept at reading new contexts for clues about tacit expectations. With changing populations and greater global connectedness, writing center workers must be adept at cultural translation. The daily work of the writing center requires us to stand outside our own worldview long enough to understand other ways of making meaning in the world. Engaging these diverse perspectives constitutes the intellectual challenge of writing center work, and frequently our heads and our hearts hurt at the end of a series of sessions. This daily work makes writing center workers acutely aware of the slippage between teachers' good intentions and students' good efforts. Our writing center encounters may make us uneasy about the regulatory role of composition and about our role in service to it, but often the literacy myth closes down opportunities to use the daily work of the writing center to rethink literacy learning for postmodern times. We convince ourselves that we are "doing good" by helping students survive academically. I believe we need to move beyond the private "doing good" model into a public effort to change society's understanding of literacy.

From a postmodern perspective, academic literacy can no longer be imagined as an unequivocally good thing, and writing center work cannot be represented as an innocent effort to help students improve their writing skills, develop their cognitive capacity, or initiate them into discourse communities. Paulo Freire spent a lifetime developing a philosophy of literacy education appropriate for cultures undergoing political and social change. Aware that an approach to literacy fostering acculturation was inadequate, he worked out a philosophy of literacy very agreeable to the challenges of postmodernity. Instead of defining literacy as a measure of one's ability to read and write, Freire defines it in terms of one's attitude and relationship with the world. According to Freire, both students and teachers (terms he avoided using because of their implied hierarchy) need to develop the "capacity for reflection, about the world, about their position in the world, about their work, about their power to transform the world, about the encounter of consciousness—about literacy itself" (1973, 81). Freire demonstrates that much of what passes as education is based on faulty conceptions of knowledge and communication. According to Freire, true knowledge is "built up in the relations between human beings and the world, relations of transformation, and perfects itself in the critical problematization of these relations" (109). Freire explains that successful educators "know that they know little (for this very reason they know that they know something) and thus can succeed in knowing more in dialogue with those who almost always think they know nothing" (99). He notes that when we teach students to adapt rather than invent, students lose the ability to make choices because their decisions result from "external prescriptions" (4). He explains that to acquire a critical literacy is to separate oneself from what is natural, to develop "a stance of intervention in one's context" (48). Freire's approach to literacy is compatible with writing center activity in a time of postmodernity because it emphasizes intersubjective knowledge built up in the relationship between people and because it questions what before was taken as natural and imagines the possibilities of transformed practices.

Postmodernity does not hold to the utopian modernist dream that we can, through a process of education, "develop" all citizens to think, act, and perform in a culturally common way. By questioning the narrative of development that is always applied to literacy—personal development, the development of critical thinking, economic development, [un]developed writers—postmodernity invites us to question the assumption that literacy always leads to improvement in cognitive capacity, in governance, in cultures, in civilization. Scholars who are thinking about literacy in postmodern times redefine literacy as the ability to translate and negotiate meaning across cultural traditions. Postmodern conditions challenge us to live with tensions and to be open to transformation. In postmodern times, literacy has less to do with strategy and prestige and more to do with the ability to make quick shifts in discourse orientation and to achieve relationships with people in different cultural systems—not by imposing a monocultural standard on them but by negotiating our differences. This kind of literacy may be more difficult to achieve than a literacy of adaptation to the dominant culture because it offers no guarantees of innocence. Even though the guarantee of innocence was based on false premises and on disguised values, it provided comfort to a vast middle class.

The New London Group, which includes international specialists in literacy and pedagogy, argues that hope for averting "catastrophic conflicts about identities and spaces" rests on a vastly different vision of literacy. Their emphasis on multiliteracies hinges on the paradox that although we inherit cultural designs, we always have opportunities in situated practice to transform rather than simply reproduce these designs. They explain that today's workers, citizens, and community members no longer benefit from a pedagogy intended to empower them in the use of "one proper, standard, or powerful language." They define literacy much more broadly in ways that acknowledge its ideological impact:

> Local diversity and global connectedness mean not only that there can be no standard; they also mean that the most important skill students need to learn is to negotiate regional, ethnic, or class-based dialects; variations in register that occur according to social context; hybrid cross-cultural discourses; the code switching often to be found within a text among different languages, dialects, or registers; different visual and iconic meanings; and variations in the gestural relationships among people, language, and material objects. (1996, 69)

Rather than cover up the social tensions that interfere with our efforts to communicate across our differences, differences that "are not as neutral, colorful, and benign as a simplistic multiculturalism might want us to believe" (89), these scholars remind us that we need to convince students and teachers that they are active participants in social change, designers of social futures.

Pretending that Mary just needs to read more of the essays in her feminist anthology and follow the assignment directions (so that she can be more like us critically literate folks who question received truths) was never an effective approach to tutoring or teaching. We need to learn to live with the paradox that Mary and many other students don't want to be like us, just as students like Mary need to come to terms with how their interactions with us and with the ideas that they encounter in their education will alter their identities. In the vision of literacy proposed by the New London Group, Mary and students like her can join with us to imagine a social future in which the vision of academic success includes a "critique of hierarchy and economic injustice" (67).

The shift in focus from individuals to culture is not a move that will make writing center practice easier. "Culture," Raymond Williams writes in *Keywords*, "is one of the two or three most complicated words in the English language" (1976, 76). He traces the complications to its "intricate historical development" in several European languages and to its use to represent different concepts in different intellectual disciplines. In all its early uses, culture was "a noun of process: the tending of something, basically crops or animals" (77). Gradually the word originally used in animal husbandry came to be used as a metaphor for human development. Williams reminds us that the complicated meanings of culture are connected to unresolved issues about the relationship between general human development and *a* particular way of life. "Virtually all the hostility" (82) surrounding the use of the word is connected to claims that one particular culture holds a superior knowledge. If we acknowledge that literacy practices recruit and construct us in ways that privilege one culture, then we need to make room in writing center practice to negotiate with those constructions. The construction that Mary faced is not unique to her or to students whose teachers use a particular kind of reading anthology, but is the pervasive regulation of middle-class subjectivity that many composition researchers have identified with composition teaching (Brodkey 1989, 1992, 1995; Faigley 1992; Helmers 1994; Miller 1991).

Taking a cue from Williams, writing center work can be redefined, so that instead of cultivating individual minds writing centers become places where tutors and students learn to negotiate with *a* culturally specific way of writing while acknowledging the culturally diverse literacies that have always been part of American life. In this approach, we must be wary of the tendency to reify or essentialize culture. Mary, who was raised without television and whose view of a committed relationship is unusual for her generation, has clearly spent time in American malls and with American fashion magazines. In spite of some strong differences, she shares much common ground with her peers and is not so culturally naive that she needs to be "helped" to understand a supposedly superior cultural attitude. Writing center people can make themselves more useful to students like Mary if they learn to articulate the tacit cultural expectations carried in academic literacy and suggest ways to negotiate with those expectations that go beyond mere acceptance or rejection.

Miles Myers (1996) has articulated the conceptualization of a new literacy in terms similar to Brandt and the New London Group. Calling attention to the need to communicate across boundaries (*translation*) while recognizing the strength of differences (*critique*), Myers defines this new conception as *translation/critical* literacy. Myers argues that literacy is never absolute but always culturally and historically contingent. As notions of mind change over time, so do notions of literacy. Myers locates the beginnings of translation/critical literacy in December 1983, the time when *A Nation at Risk* was published, and the public began to debate the educational standards that would enable workers to manage technological change and keep the United States competitive in world markets. A more flexible understanding of literacy was needed, one that allowed for understanding patterns of intention shaped by cultural interactions. Like Brandt, Myers acknowledges the importance of using older forms of literacy to make the transition to understanding newer forms. Drawing on the work of Bernstein and Delpit, he also notes that "translation/critical literacy's flexible, negotiating attitude in teaching style may make the new literacy incomprehensible and possibly invisible to students from a social class more accustomed to decoding/analytic distinctions" (299). To provide orientation, Myers says we "may need to teach some of the history of our differences" (299).

In the absence of promises of innocence, writing center people can make effective use of their daily encounters with differences of gender, ethnicity, religion, race, and class by learning to articulate the diverse worldviews that are linked to difference and to develop a diverse array of communicative practices that allow participants to translate and negotiate as they account for differences. Composition theorist Joseph Harris, reflecting on composition's embrace of a contact zone metaphor, worries that "what is missing from such descriptions of the contact zone is a sense of how competing perspectives can be made to intersect with and inform each other" as well as a sense of "how (or why) individuals might decide to change or revise their own positions (rather than simply to defend them) when brought into contact with differing views" (1997, 119). If writing centers move away from positions that support the literacy myth, they are well situated to reflect on what happens when perspectives intersect and inform each other.

Many of us who work in writing centers have learned to negotiate the tensions of competing perspectives because in a writing center environment identities are fluid, criteria for evaluation are temporarily suspended, and interaction is one-to-one. In fact, effectiveness as writing coaches depends on our ability to "at once, see through serpent and eagle eyes" (Anzaldua 1987, 78). In my work with Rebecca, for example, I reenter the perspective of the working-class student, and I re-experience the conflicts between the desire of "wanting in" with the anger at being "kept out." Through this double perspective, I reclaim some of what I left behind and gain more awareness of what it took to get in. I notice that Rebecca's habits of directness, which stand in contrast to the elaborate hedging of middle-class practices, make her a good writing coach, and I reclaim that directness. If I learn from Rebecca's compassionate response to people *and* her detachment from the institution, I find committee meetings less draining. In contact with Rebecca, I change who I am and how I direct the writing center. I revise the training manual to reflect a less prescriptive and more strongly narrative-based approach to tutoring, one that I hope encourages our writing coaches to enter into exploratory discussion with students whose experiences they do not share. In a similar fashion, Rebecca also changes, claiming confidence previously denied her in school settings, learning that her challenging questions not only are valid but also, in some instances, have an effect on institutional practices.

The positioning and repositioning metaphor that underlies so much recent scholarship on literacy suggests the fluid movements of dance and athletics, metaphors familiar to many students. These metaphors of fluidity offer alternative ways to think of identity conflicts that seem unresolvable in modernist understandings of literacy. In contrast to modernist metaphors that construct students as "developing" writers, postmodern notions of literacy focus on the game, the moves, the orientations—all of which encourage a more flexible, even playful, understanding of communicating and identity construction. For example, playing the position of right wing on the hockey team does not fundamentally alter one's identity. Right wing is a fluid offensive position, a good wing reads the game, shifting to a defensive position when the situation calls for it. Success—whether as a hockey player, a dancer, or a postmodern communicator—requires this ability to read the game, to make quick shifts in orientation and positioning. Rather than hide behind a guarantee of innocence, and operate in ignorance of the history, culture, and social relationships that are ignored by autonomous literacy, writing centers can foreground cultural conflicts for students and render visible to the field of composition studies the literacies and conflicts "forgotten" by the autonomous model. Rather than simply manage the status quo, writing centers can be places where students learn to orient themselves to the literacy challenges of postmodern cultural change.

Translation/critical literacy requires learners and teachers to juxtapose different languages, discourses, styles, and approaches. This juxtaposition develops meta-cognitive and meta-linguistic abilities as well as the ability to "reflect critically on complex systems and their interactions" (New London Group 1996, 69). Because writing center people operate "at the border" or crossroads of multiple literacies—the ones students bring to college, the ones their teachers expect them to demonstrate, the ones practiced in discourses across disciplines—our daily practice develops the ability to make these quick shifts and juxtapositions. This ability to juxtapose is a tacit knowing, developed from exposure to differences in expectations. Postmodern understandings of literacy create the opportunity and the ethical responsibility to make this tacit knowing explicit. When writing center people learn to think aloud as they read drafts, juxtaposing competing responses for writers to see and hear, they can then assist students in learning positions, in seeing possibilities for redesign, in mapping the cultural tensions that are carried in competing notions of literacy. Meta-discursive fluency— the ability to recognize and articulate the different values, expectations, and habits of mind that underlie competing cultural notions of literacy—is a skill that most effective writing center workers develop without conscious awareness. It is this very skill that is most needed for postmodern literacy.

Writing centers have much to gain from an understanding of the literacy competencies that will meet the challenges of postmodern social change. In fact, these changes create possibilities for writing centers to use the knowledge made in everyday interactions. Because modernist models of literacy emphasized features of written academic texts, they deemphasized the social and interpersonal function of language and distanced readers from texts, speakers from listeners. Within modernist models, the rationality and logic of the text, rather than its usefulness or comprehensibility in everyday life, was the sole criteria for judging its effectiveness. Postmodern models of literacy allow writing centers to make use of the transformative understandings that have always resulted from daily writing center face-to-face interactions yet were often never articulated.

Many writing center practitioners know their lives have been transformed by the understandings they developed in writing centers. These are the literacy workers who operate not with the righteousness of a missionary or the innocence of a tourist or the pedigree of educational privilege but with the imagination, curiosity, and humility of people open to listening and incorporating alternative wisdom and perspectives. In postmodern times, our hope for deeply democratic institutions will rest on the development of our ability to listen, a communicative capacity overlooked in modernist culture. Philosopher Gemma Corradi Fiumara comments that "humans who 'logically' always aspire to 'be right,' no longer have the strength to free themselves from a contaminated language that may become hypertrophic and misleading: a language that is no longer an instrument of communicative coexistence" (1990, 197). If Fiumara is right that the discourses of rationality, which enabled us to control reality, are no longer adequate for survival, then in order to open new horizons in literacy learning we need first to open ourselves to the transformative potential of authentic listening.

An understanding of literacy as cultural practice doesn't offer a promise of innocence or right answers; rather, it challenges us to theorize our practice in the context of the specific cultural differences, localities, and politics (Street 1995). Moreover, it challenges us to call attention to the cultural assumptions and power relations involved rather than ignore them, to understand and question the history and the culture that position us to "help" others, to open ourselves to ideological contest rather than assume that our well-intentioned practices are innocent. In the age of postmodernity, writing center practitioners can work with students, not to lead them into the light of literacy but instead to shine a light on how literacy works as a cultural practice. When we understand that students' lived experiences are not accounted for in the subjectivities they are expected to assume in university writing assignments, we can locate the problem in social conflict rather than in inadequate and undeveloped student writers, and we can offer students more choices so that they can be agents rather than subjects of literacy practices. By placing writing center work fully within the paradox of literacy, we can access the transformative potential of working at the liminal intersections of literacies.

Note

1. In the middle of Rebecca's first term at the university, Marsha Penti, a writing center colleague, and I asked her to participate in a research project that looked at the experience of rural working-class students in a cultural studies-based composition course. Rebecca was one of two students who worked with us in an extensive exploration of the literacy histories such students bring to college. This study is reported in Grimm and Penti (1998).

Chapter Three

Redesigning Academic Identity Kits[1]

Figuring out what the teacher wants and performing the expected role is often the expedient academic strategy for students. In fact, it happens so often that it seems the normal thing to do. Jim Berlin related this story of how he learned to play the academic identity game.

> OK, when I was an undergraduate, I was told in my 101 course that I must "reveal more of myself," I must present "my feelings." At the time, I remember, we were reading *The Catcher in the Rye*, writing about Holden Caulfield. And so what I did was, I said that I identified with Holden Caulfield, that I often felt the way he did, and I presented this persona that I was manufacturing because my professor said that I was supposed to "tell more about myself." But I knew that what he really wanted was for me to sound like Holden Caulfield, not like myself at all. That was his notion of a sensitive adolescent, and if I was going to please him, I was going to have to do that. Now, I was a working-class, somewhat streetwise kid from Detroit, and I knew that I wasn't revealing myself to him. I was creating a persona. I wasn't going to tell that guy what I really felt. If I'd told him what I really felt about Holden Caulfield at that time, I probably would've gotten an F—and he would have been deeply hurt. (*laughter*) Really, I mean, here I was a working-class kid, a Catholic, and the things that Holden Caulfield did really upset me. But I told him what he wanted to hear. (McDonald 1994, 34)

Telling the teacher what she or he "wants to hear" and doing it under the pressure of a deadline often means picking a safe topic and avoiding any issues that are difficult to resolve.

Berlin's story prompted memories of an essay about male and female roles that I wrote in my 101 class, long before gender became an issue in the academy, before the formation of the National Organization for Women, even before the publication of *Ms.* magazine. To my surprise, my essay gained enough positive attention that one of my classmates, an editor for the college newspaper, wanted to publish it. It was an "if,then" piece: reacting against the cultural assumptions of the times but unable to think beyond them, I argued that *if* women were expected to assume subservient roles, *then* men better learn to be more assertive. To this day the essay still embarrasses me. I was supposed to write an argument, and it was clear that my teacher liked strong conclusions. Although I used incidents from my experience to produce the essay, my conclusion was far removed from what I believed. None of the meandering, unfocused, and contradictory pieces that I had written previously in that class received the positive attention that this piece did. I learned that writing well meant projecting certainty and confidence and clarity. Shortly after, I changed my major from journalism, where I was expected to write confident accounts of events, to English literature, where I could hide behind experienced critics.

Thirty years later I find myself directing a writing center and still wrestling with composition's efforts to regulate not only a white middle-class identity but also a coherent and unconflicted identity. The modernist evaluation criteria of clarity, coherence, and focus do not readily encourage students to explore the slippage between the identity their assignments call for and the identities formed by their lived experiences. Successful students learn what Linda Brodkey calls the fluency trick: they look for a subject "simple enough that it can *appear* to be adequately elaborated and naturally resolved in the requisite number of words" (1995, 222). As Brodkey explains, "Fluency is dangerous because it assumes there to be a necessary and positive correlation between *clear* writing and *clear* thinking, which any honest student can tell you is patently not the case" (222). Like Joe, who tries to reconcile his experience growing up on a mink farm with popular press accounts of the arguments of animal rights activists, and Mary, who brings an unexpected religious identity into contact with a composition assignment, students often take the easy way out: either they eliminate that which creates complexity as Joe did or they offer an account of themselves that is unaffected by the complicated issues under examination in their class, as Mary did. I don't believe teachers intend for this to happen; in fact, I suspect most teachers are unaware that their assignments serve to regulate a certain kind of identity for students.

In this chapter, I look at the process of social regulation in order to identify ways that writing center workers might intervene in it. My aim is to move writing center practice in the direction of a literacy of the contact zone by focusing on the conceptual stumbling blocks to that move, particularly the social pressures that keep the academic identity kit intact. I don't intend to rescue agency and identity from postmodern challenges but to move further into them and reckon with the realization that literacy learning is often far from the liberating experience that we like to imagine. First, I show how the "normal" ideological assumptions of composition leave little room for negotiating individual class and racial identities. Then, I examine an essay about a tutorial interaction written by Anne DiPardo, "'Whispers of Coming and Going': Lessons from Fannie," to illustrate the extent to which individuals internalize the habits of social regulation. Finally, I reexamine the same essay to show how postmodern theories of subjectivity can suggest possibilities for changed relationships in which students "see themselves as active participants in social change . . . [as] active designers . . . of social futures" (New London Group 1996, 64).

Within a modernist framework, we often imagine ourselves as agents when we succeed in conforming to social regulation. In the writing center, for example, students and their tutors often work to make papers match the assignments constructed by teachers rather than design new genres. As Marilyn Cooper has observed, it is really quite irrational to believe that in matching the specifications of the assignment, students are learning to exercise agency in writing or take ownership of texts (1994, 102). Cooper argues that writing centers, because of their close contact with institutional regulation *and* with students' lived experiences, are well positioned "to develop new templates for texts" and to identify "what spaces are left open" for the construction of different subject positions (109). Before writing center workers can take advantage of Cooper's suggestion, they need to understand how social regulation works. Negotiating with social norms requires a willingness to scrutinize one's own implication in cultural power, which is not a task for the faint of heart.

Composition, like most disciplines, functions with a particular ideology, a set of tightly linked expectations about beliefs, thoughts, and values that are assumed to be not only "right" but "normal." These beliefs about identity are always embedded within a Discourse, a word that is often capitalized and used to signal "the inescapably political contexts in which we speak and work" (Apple quoted in Lather 1991, vii). As James Gee puts it, "Each Discourse protects itself by demanding from its adherents performances which act as though its ways of being, thinking, acting, talking, writing, reading, and valuing are right, natural, obvious, the way good and intelligent and normal people behave" (1996, 190–91). When someone writes or talks in ways that do not conform to those expectations, those inside the Discourse think of them as "not normal" or "wrong." Thus, literacy teaching often functions in hegemonic ways to maintain the social order. Because teachers and tutors function within a discourse, they are often unaware when their practices discriminate against students with differences of race, class, religion, sexual orientation, culture, or ethnicity. Educational discourse (and the discourse of composition studies) is implicated in the American belief in meritocracy. Education is supposed to guarantee equal opportunity to all individuals who work hard, so we often "forget" that literacy learning is not always a happy march of individual progress but really a matter of conforming to predetermined expectations which are, for better or worse, set by the dominant white middle-class culture.

As a writing center tutor, I have worked with many students who have struggled with the social norm identified by their assignments. Hajj, an African American student, whitens the dialect in his narrative to earn the grade he needs; Rebecca distrusts her teacher's encouragement to write from her experience because too often her working-class experience has prejudiced teachers against her; Nancy, a Latina in a dominantly Anglo institution, struggles to write a master's thesis because she is not comfortable positioning herself as an insider, nor is she comfortable drawing on the "outsider" cultural knowledge that informs her interpretations. When students cannot find ways to integrate their nonmainstream perspectives, academic writing becomes a lifeless performance, and they construct writing positions they do not believe in. Because universities reward and punish academic behaviors with grades and because corporations later use grades to make hiring decisions, students seem to have no choice but to conform. If students decide to resist regulation, teachers say they will "hurt themselves in the long run" because they will "earn" poor grades.

Constructing a position to match the one in the teacher's head is not in itself a bad thing to do. The strategy of figuring out what the teacher wants can serve students well, particularly when they are writing under the pressure of a deadline and with no compelling motivation of their own. People often decide to conform to others' expectations, or, to put a more positive spin on it, to "play the game." In fact, this can be a way to practice rhetorical skills, learning to shape a message for a particular audience. However, when this strategy is the only one available to students, our classrooms and writing centers are not places where students are learning the arts of the contact zone. As Mary Louise Pratt observes, when the *legitimate* moves, strategies, games, and scripts are always defined by those in power, the classroom becomes "a world homogenized with respect to the teacher" (1991, 38). If literate ability is redefined as the ability to negotiate differences, to juxtapose different languages, discourses, and styles, to translate across boundaries, and to communicate with awareness of the history of differences that structure our interactions with one another, then teachers and students in a seemingly homogenized classroom lose valuable opportunities to imagine a different future and to develop the skills of negotiation and translation.

My desire for change in the way literacy is practiced in the writing center is not motivated by pity for the predicaments of students who are not mainstream but rather by concern about the impoverished sense of self that comes from ignoring voices outside our own reality. In my work with students like Mary, Hajj, Joe, Rebecca, and Nancy, I have learned to see the culture that informs my thinking, a culture previously invisible because of the processes of naturalization.

Cultural Denial, or, Let's Pretend Identity Regulation Doesn't Happen

Our intensely individualistic culture compels us to deny the mutual interdependence between the individual and the social, the ways we constitute one another intersubjectively and relationally. In composition teaching many of our practices depend upon understanding students and teachers as completely autonomous individuals, unaffected by unconscious needs, the desires of others, or social regulation. When composition students are imagined to be freely choosing individuals, the cultural conflicts they experience as they attempt to comply with the expectations are overlooked. This cultural denial creates many contradictions in writing center work. When writing center workers posit the "individual" as the center of their work, they attempt to indirectly "regulate" that individual to conform to the expectations. If the individual "resists" efforts at regulation, tutors become frustrated because the student rejects their help. On the other hand, if the individual signs up for an excessive number of appointments or "tries to get the tutor to do his work for him," they worry that this excessive use of the writing center might not be ethical, and they complain that the student is "not taking responsibility" because he or she is taking advantage of "too much" social regulation.

Even when we acknowledge that the beliefs of the dominant culture form the basis for much of what we do in composition, the tendency is to defend this as a good and inevitable practice. Lynn Bloom's essay, "Freshman Composition as a Middle-Class Enterprise," provides an excellent example of the rationale teachers use to justify the normal way of teaching composition. With good wit and good scholarship, Bloom acknowledges that freshman composition is "an unabashedly middle-class enterprise" that has the worthy aim of enabling students "to think and write in ways that will make them good citizens of the academic (and larger) community, and viable candidates for good jobs upon graduation" (1996, 655). Bloom believes that most of the time, this middle-class orientation operates for the better because middle-class values and virtues promote the well-being of America's "vast middle class." They operate for the worse when "middle-class teachers punish lower-class students for not being, well, more middle class" (655). Through an analysis of rhetorical history and composition and style texts, Bloom illustrates how virtues promoted by Benjamin Franklin—self-reliance, respectability, decorum, moderation, thrift, efficiency, order, cleanliness, punctuality, and delayed gratification—have become a template for the aims of composition teaching. According to Bloom, freshman composition functions like the "chlorine footbath" at the neighborhood swimming pool; it is an enterprise in which "students' vices must be eradicated" and where they are "indoctrinated against further transgressions" (656). The footbath metaphor and the vice/virtue binary imply that the middle class is middle class because they are more virtuous than the working class or the poor or the unemployed, and thus deserving of being recognized as the dominant culture.

After illustrating the extent to which middle-class values saturate the pedagogy of composition teaching, Bloom concludes her essay by examining an alternative argument—one that suggests that literacy practices alone do not account for a rise in status to the middle class. She looks at John Trimbur's work, for example, and his argument that narratives about the transformative power of literacy reproduce the myth that the unequal distribution of goods is a matter of individual effort and talent rather than systematic inequality. After considering Trimbur's and others' arguments against the literacy myth, Bloom observes, "The views of Trimbur, Stuckey, France, and other academic Marxists notwithstanding, such stories [the literacy autobiographies written by diverse authors such as Mike Rose, Frederick Douglass, Maya Angelou, and Maxine Hong Kingston] embody what American education has historically been dedicated to—not putting the 'finishing' veneer on an elite class, but enabling the transformation and mobility of lives across boundaries, from the margins to the mainstreams of success and assimilation on middle-class terms" (668). In spite of her awareness of the critiques of the literacy myth, Bloom clearly prefers linking literacy with meritocratic success. She comments "like it or not, despite the critiques of academic Marxists, we are a nation of Standard English" (670). Bloom hopes, however, that teachers will make it an ethical and cultural obligation "to respect the world's multiple ways of living and speaking" while they are teaching the dominant standard (671).

Most white middle-class people would find Bloom's argument reasonable. She acknowledges that this nation values Standard English; she believes students are well served by learning the standard;

she believes that people who learn the standard can move from the margins to the mainstream; and she insists that teachers respect their students no matter what variety of English they speak as they learn. How could anyone object to such a culturally realistic and culturally sensitive argument as Bloom's? At a time when other scholars are undermining middle-class values, Bloom's historical tracing makes these values seem innocent and wholesome. Who wouldn't be well served by developing these American cultural habits?

Surprising things happen when one begins to articulate the tacit values and assumptions that underlie composition practices. I am thankful for Bloom's rendering of composition's values, but at the same time I must admit I was more than annoyed on my first reading. From the time we were children and well into our professional lives, both Bloom and I have been aware of the way class manifests itself in the clothes people wear, the language they speak, or the choices they make. Yet Bloom lived within the naturalized world and material comforts of the middle class, with the belief that all those Franklinesque virtues belonged to her class, while I always believed that money, not virtue, determined social class.

Bloom appears to be claiming for her class many of the values that were practiced in my working-class family. The socks in my family were worn too thin, not because we were slovenly but because my mother practiced thrift, buying our shoes a size too big, stuffing cotton in the toes so they would last longer before we outgrew them. (In spite of the cotton—or maybe because of it—the shoes rubbed the backs of our socks.) It took a great deal of efficiency and order on my mother's part to sew school clothes for three daughters. We went into debt during holidays so that our family could arrive at church dressed in a respectable and decorous fashion. Self-reliance, drilled into me, my brother, and two sisters from the time we were old enough to apply for a work permit, is what got all four of us through college. Punctuality cannot be fudged when fourteen-year-olds are slipping their time cards into a time clock. Delayed gratification enabled us to pay off government loans after graduation. Those virtues extolled by Ben Franklin were not only enacted in our family's lifestyle, but both my parents, neither of whom had more than a high school education, also regularly applied these virtues to written work—letters to family and friends, notes to teachers, family memoirs, personal poetry, and journal entries. In other words, literacy (and what some consider its attendant virtues) was valued in my family, and we were still working class.

Bloom notes that although class forms the basis for much of what is expected of composition, it has been until very recently an invisible issue. She tells how when she was chair of the MLA Division of Teaching Writing in 1993, she issued a call for papers on race, class, and gender in composition studies, and "received only one proposal on class—in comparison with a dozen on race and ninety-four on gender" (1996, 657). She does not note, however, that the MLA has been traditionally associated with high-brow culture or that it is an expensive conference held during the Christmas holidays, a time of budget strain for families that are not middle class. One of the assumptions that Bloom seems to make is that all college teachers are protected from the material realities of class. And to some extent she is right. Because of my education, I no longer punch a time clock nor do I hesitate to buy well-fitting shoes and new socks. Because of our advanced degrees, my husband (also of working-class origin) and I have raised two children in middle-class circumstances.

Nevertheless, the comforts of my middle-class position are not so powerful that they erase memory. Bloom's stories about her middle-class upbringing as the daughter of a college professor in a small New Hampshire town stir up my neighborhood and school memories. Like Bloom, I went to an elementary school where the social classes came in contact with one another, but unlike Bloom, I was not a member of the vast middle class. Bloom says that in her family class was never an issue until she "started dating boys her parents didn't approve of" (657). Those boys that Bloom's parents disapproved of (such as the one-time boyfriend who "said 'ain't,' and wore too-tight jeans" (658) could have been my neighbors—or my brother. Class was never an issue in my family, either, until the middle-class parents of my school friends raised concerned eyebrows when I responded to their questions about where I lived. Although Bloom and I may be near the same age (I, too, wore full skirts and blouses with Peter Pan collars, but mine were homemade, even the one with the felt poodle appliqué), Bloom writes her essay from a full-professor position in a chair underwritten by an insurance company, and I write mine from an untenured assistant professor position, having earned a doctorate in middle age.

"Watch it," I tell myself, "You may be projecting too much of your own baggage onto Bloom." Certainly, the humor of Bloom's essay comes from her refusal to be apologetic for her middle-class values, and the chippiness of my reaction comes from my experience of growing up in a working-class family. Nevertheless, the material circumstances of one's childhood have a strong impact on identity formation, and the assumptions of composition don't seem to take those circumstances into consideration. The cultural denial of class memory exemplified in Bloom's mutually exclusive categories of "we middle-class teachers" and "academic Marxists" excludes those of us whose approach to composition is informed by working-class memories, memories reinforced perhaps by "academic" perspectives, but rooted in experience that Bloom and other middle-class teachers haven't shared. The argument that as a middle-class enterprise, composition intends the best for students and their future success doesn't make room for the cultural conflicts created when class, racial, or ethnic memories meet up with assumptions about the Normal middle-class way of doing things.

Because of the way middle-class assumptions inform schooling as a whole and not just composition teaching, many students never learn the historical context of their personal memories. Historian James W. Loewen speculates "If the 'we' in a [history] textbook included American Indians, African Americans, Latinos, women, and all social classes, the book would read differently, just as whites talk differently (and more humanely) in the presence of people of color" (1995, 296). In *Lies My Teacher Told Me*, Loewen argues that the familiar cultural theme of history textbooks—America as the Land of Opportunity—is responsible for the ignorance of many Americans about the existence of class and social structure. Class is kept an invisible issue because it contradicts the "our great country" story. Loewen's research shows that history books rarely mention social class even when they discuss labor history (195). Loewen observes that even though Americans like to think we have less class stratification than other countries, "in Japan, the average chief executive officer in an automobile manufacturing firm makes twenty times as much as the average worker in an automobile assembly plant; in the United States he (and it is not she) makes 192 times as much" (203). According to Loewen, portraying America as a hero without faults means leaving out the fact that 1 percent of our population controls 40 percent of our wealth.

When he interviewed the social studies and history editor in one of the biggest textbook publishing firms about this omitted topic, Loewen was told, "You always run the risk, if you talk about social class, of being labeled Marxist" (205). Loewen concludes that the America-as-land-of-social-equality-and-opportunity story creates the false impression that "folks get what they deserve and deserve what they get, the failures of working-class Americans to transcend their class origin inevitably get laid at their own doorsteps" (201). Because alternative narratives are not offered in school, working-class students have no way to explain their family's position, and they can develop a "subculture of shame." The opinions of working-class students are often silenced with the "if you're so smart, why aren't you rich?" assumption, sometimes unspoken and sometimes not. To illustrate the effect that truncated versions of history have on affluent white children, Loewen uses what he calls the "Vietnam exercise." He has invited more than a thousand college students, generally members of his audiences, to indicate their beliefs about which kind of adults, by educational level, supported the Vietnam War. He usually finds that ten to one, audience members believe that educated Americans were more likely to have supported withdrawal based on their hypotheses that educated people are more critical, informed, and tolerant. In fact, polls taken during the war showed again and again that college-educated Americans were more hawkish. Richard Hamilton is another historian who has shown that many outbreaks of authoritarianism and intolerance such as Nazism, lynchings in the American South, and McCarthyism, were initiated by the wealthy and better educated (Ehrenreich 1989, 110).

To explain why so many believed that educated Americans would not have supported the Vietnam War, Loewen identifies two social processes that occur in school that he calls allegiance and socialization. As he explains it, in America we are taught in school to believe that one earns successful positions through virtuous behavior and individual characteristics rather than through one's parents' social position. As a result, educated adults "have a vested interest in believing that the society that helped them be educated and successful is fair" and thus they "are more likely to show allegiance to society" than to be critical of it (1995, 301). Education socializes us to believe in the rightness of our society, so "the more school, the more socialization, and the more likely the individual will conclude that America is good" (301). As Loewen indicates, the social processes of schools make it difficult for the middle class to think critically about their own positions. Their perceptions have been dominant for so long that they are naturalized. It becomes difficult for them to be aware of their own "otherness"; whiteness and middle income seem to be the norm and everything else is "cultural."

As Barbara Ehrenreich explains in her book *Fear of Falling,* the only "capital" of the middle class is "knowledge and skill, or at least the credentials imputing skill and knowledge. And unlike real capital, these cannot be hoarded against hard times" (1989, 15). Ehrenreich theorizes that the middle class occupies a tenuous position, beset by "fear of inner weakness, of growing soft, of failing to strive, of losing discipline and will" (15). Because these fears are not openly acknowledged, they become inner anxieties that are projected onto the working class. The middle class is prone to depict the working class as tacky, slothful, and ignorant people who eat white bread and Twinkies, drink Budweiser, and live in tract houses. In my local grocery store, Budweiser costs $3.85 a six-pack compared to $7.19 for imported beers like Heineken and Corona, but rarely is the cost of things a factor in judgments the middle class makes about taste, including judgments about too-tight clothing and worn socks. Professional middle-class people display their status through consumption, and because capitalism encourages endless consumption, the middle class must consume more to maintain their status. Increased consumption threatens the necessary middle-class virtues, especially delayed gratification and thrift, and so the inner anxiety is perpetuated and seeks relief in displacement.

According to Ehrenreich, the university operates as the "core institution" of the middle class; it is "the employer of its intellectual elite and producer of the next generation of middle-class, professional personnel" (58). The routines of university life create structures that prohibit the contributions of outsiders, and university life becomes infused with "the delusion of 'knowing it all'" (140). Because the professional middle class is based on expertise, much of what universities produce are people in the helping professions—teachers, doctors, social workers. Ehrenreich observes, "Within its fortress of 'expertise,' the middle class imagines it is the sole repository of useful information—even information about the lives of those who dwell outside the moats." She illustrates by quoting an observation in a sociology text: "the working-class person 'often fails to realize that his story is neither understandable nor interesting to the other person'" (140). Although middle-class professionals are often generous-spirited people, Ehrenreich notes that their roles

> confer authority and the power to make judgments about others. The teacher will determine whether your child's difficulties stem from a behavior problem, a learning disability, or a simple lack of effort. The social worker, who may have vastly different notions of what constitutes "normal" family life, will scrutinize and diagnose your intimate problems. The physician will pass judgments on your habits and life style; he or she will very likely also treat you (if you are [a] poor or working-class patient) in an unconsciously patronizing or condescending manner. (139)

Ehrenreich observes, "There is simply no way for the working-class or poor person to capture the attention of middle-class personnel without seeming rude or insubordinate. In the imposed silence of working-class life, hostility thrives" (139). Reading this, I remember Rebecca telling me about her frustration with a particular math course. Her attention at lectures, her use of the math learning center, and her own diligence had not resulted in increased understanding, so she went to office hours and said to the professor, "Look, I don't understand this and you've got to teach it to me!" The ensuing interaction did not go well, as the professor interpreted Rebecca's intense desire to learn as a rude demand on him. The hard-earned tuition money that Rebecca exchanged for her education might never have entered the teacher's mind, but in Rebecca's mind she was paying in order to learn, and she wanted the teacher to explain the concept in a way that she could understand it. She was not behaving like a Normal student, content to walk through the chlorine footbath.

Because schools are run by the professional middle class, because Americans believe in individual freedom and equal opportunity, because class is a hidden issue in America, and because fears are denied and projected, the white middle-class practices of school become the Normal way of things. The middle-class assumptions of American schools allow it to function like a flattering mirror, reflecting back a comforting image of "people like us."

"Lessons from Fannie"

Anne DiPardo's essay, "'Whispers of Coming and Going': Lessons from Fannie," illustrates the consequences of the white middle-class assumptions of schooling and composition teaching. In this evocative and haunting writing center story, DiPardo analyzes the tutorial relationship between Fannie, a Navajo student, and Morgan, an African American tutor. Given that Fannie and Morgan are both what John Ogbu (1987) would call involuntary minority students,[2] one might expect that their differing non-Anglo identities might affect the ways they interact, and that Morgan might operate out of a different set of assumptions than do majority tutors. Instead, as DiPardo examines their work together, it is easy for most white middle-class tutors to identify with Morgan, the idealistic tutor eager to "spark" something in Fannie. If not for DiPardo's careful weaving of demographic data and personal detail, one could assume that Fannie was a quiet Anglo student and Morgan a sincere white middle-class tutor in the Anywhere Writing Center. Morgan is motivated by a desire to make a difference in Fannie's academic work, and she struggles with her impulse to take over Fannie's work and with her frustration when Fannie fails to respond to her coaching. The story is haunting because DiPardo allows us to see how much doesn't happen in these well-intentioned efforts and how implicated the middle-class values are in institutional silencing.

The story takes place in a basic writing tutorial program at a West Coast university. The semester-long relationship was not particularly helpful to Fannie, who barely passed her basic writing course and who expected to experience even more difficulty in her composition class. Morgan, who was preparing to become an English teacher, was full of good intentions and idealism, yet she missed many subtle clues in Fannie's sparse and reluctant contributions. She learned too late, for example, that Fannie's first language was not English and that Fannie had been raised on a reservation. It seems that many of the missed opportunities occurred paradoxically because Morgan wanted to be effective, to be mainstream, to apply strategies she learned in her classes and at a Conference on College Composition and Communication (CCCC) workshop. She was so strongly interpellated by the professional role that she was, as DiPardo writes, "insufficiently curious" about Fannie (1992, 138). Morgan could see what she wanted Fannie to become, but she couldn't see Fannie. Having internalized the process of social regulation, Morgan felt compelled to renew the status quo. DiPardo speculates that Morgan's own racial ambivalence (she responded to more racially sensitive students that she was "first and foremost a member of the *human* race"), combined with her desire to be helpful, contributed to the many missed opportunities for learning more about Fannie (133). When Fannie failed to respond to her well-intentioned efforts, Morgan attributed Fannie's writing block to her cultural background, stating assumptions about Navajo women that DiPardo shows are contrary to published accounts of Navajo life and even to Fannie's demeanor when interacting with other native students.

It is not fair to blame Morgan, an undergraduate herself, for not having more knowledge or curiosity. Raymond Williams reminds us that social regulation "is never only the setting of limits; it is also the exertion of pressures." As these pressures are internalized, they create "a compulsion to act in ways that maintain and renew" the status quo (1977, 87). Under institutional pressure to perform, to be a good tutor, to use effective strategies advocated in professional workshops, and to be a member of the *human* race, Morgan channeled her enthusiasm in a predictable direction. But what if Morgan had been prepared differently? What if her tutor training and her preprofessional education had insisted on conceptual and theoretical understanding over strategic know-how? What if she had been provided the support for sustaining anxiety and questioning her effectiveness, for turning the lens back on herself at moments of frustration? What if she had been taught first to ask if her desire to be a good teacher/tutor was being projected onto the student in ways that foreclosed learning for both of them? Because social pressures are internalized, our first response to frustration should be to look inside rather than to direct the gaze externally, but usually we don't. White middle-class practices are so Normal that we are incapable of regarding ourselves as Other.

Madeline Grumet writes that "by arranging students in rows, all eyes facing front, directly confronting the back of a fellow's head, meeting the gaze only of the teacher, the discipline of the contemporary classroom deploys the look as a strategy of domination" (1988, 111). Even though we sit next to our students in writing centers and form the chairs into a circle in our classrooms, we and our students have internalized the institutional gaze as "endorsed with an authority that disclaims history, motives and politics" (112). Under that gaze, "we expect to grow into a self within [the teacher's] look. But we always suspect that he is actually looking not at us but at another whom we do not know but who is finally more powerful and compelling than we" (125). Grumet argues that to teach well, teachers must first study the transferences they bring to their work rather than "compel students to recite the history and future of our desire" (128). She challenges teachers to "come to terms with [their] own versions of truth and with the designations [they] reserv[e] for those accounts that contradict the current wisdom" (163).

Because the power of institutional regulation is internalized and because we are most susceptible when we are anxious raw beginners like Morgan, tutor and teacher development programs need to work especially hard to cultivate the psychic space that encourages tutors to turn away from the institutional gaze, to question institutional interpellation, to develop awareness of the ways they have internalized the belief that a particular form of discourse is "right" or "natural" or "better," and that those who depart from this form are "wrong" or "not normal" or "culturally deprived." DiPardo concludes, "Rather than frequent urgings to 'talk less,' perhaps what Morgan most needed was advice to listen more—for the clues students like Fannie would provide, for those moments when she might best shed her persona and become once again a learner" (1992, 140).

DiPardo's sage advice is difficult to achieve because we live in a "non-listening culture." According to Fiumara (1990), authentic listening occurs only when "an embryonic thought is protected from the restrictive interference of over-zealous classification" (161), yet in tutoring interactions, listening is often done under the pressure of time, usually with a desire to be helpful, and almost always with a notion of what is a normal academic essay. As Fannie struggled to connect her class assignments with her Native American heritage, she decided to write about the environment. In the following transcript, Fannie looks for words to express her connection with the land, and Morgan, unable to restrain the desire to be helpful, misses clues to Fannie's meaning as she encourages Fannie to focus:

Morgan: What would you say your basic theme is? And sometimes if you keep that in mind, then you can always, you know, keep that as a focus for what you're writing. And the reason I say that is 'cause when you say, "well living happily wasn't. . . ."

Fannie: (*pause*) . . . Well, America was a beautiful country, well, but it isn't beautiful anymore.

Morgan: Um-hm. Not as beautiful.

Fannie: So I should just say, America was a beautiful country?

Morgan: Yeah. But I dunno—what do you think your overall theme is, that you're saying?

Fannie: (*long pause*) . . . I'm really, I'm just talking about America.

Morgan: America? So America as . . . ?

Fannie: (*pause*) . . . Um . . . (*pause*)

Morgan: Land of free, uh, land of natural resources? As, um, a place where there's a conflict, I mean, there, if you can narrow that, "America." What is it specifically, and think about what you've written, in the rest. Know what I mean?

Fannie: (*pause*) . . . The riches of America, or the country? I don't know . . .

Morgan: I think you do. I'm not saying there's any right answer, but I, I'm— for me, the reason I'm saying this, is I see this emerging as, you know, (*pause*) where you're really having a hard time with dealing with the exploitation that you see, of America, you know, you think that. And you're using two groups to really illustrate, specifically, how two different attitudes toward, um, the richness and beauty of America, two different, um, ways people have to approach this land. Does that, does this make any sense? Or am I just putting words in your mouth? I don't want to do that. I mean that's what I see emerge in your paper. But I could be way off base.

Fannie: I think I know what you're trying to say. And I can kind of relate it at times to what I'm trying to say.

Morgan: You know, I mean, this is like the theme I'm picking up . . . (*pause*) I think you know, you've got some real, you know, environmental issues here. I think you're a closet environmentalist here. Which are real true, know what I mean? (*pause*) And when you talk about pollution, and waste, and, um, those types of things. So I mean, if you're looking at a theme of your paper, what could you pick out, of something of your underlying theme.

Fannie: (*pause*) . . . The resources, I guess?

Morgan: Well, I mean, I don't want you to say, I want you to say, don't say "I guess," is that what you're talking about?

Fannie: Yeah.

Morgan: "Yeah?" I mean, it's your paper.

Fannie: I know, I want to talk about the land. . . .

Morgan: OK. So you want to talk about the land, and the beauty of the land . . .

Fannie: Um-hm.

Morgan: . . . and then, um, and then also your topic for your, um, to spark your paper . . . what values, and morals, right? That's where you based off to write about America, and the land, you know. Maybe you can write some of these things down, as we're talking, as focusing things, you know. So you want to talk about the land, and then it's like, what do you want to say about the land? (Dipardo 1992, 135–36)

Morgan, in her desire to "spark" something, pushes Fannie toward writing about commonplace environmental concerns; she doesn't recognize the theme Fannie wants to write about (even though Fannie asserts it twice), and she knows what sorts of themes are usually addressed in an academic essay. Morgan was quick to classify Fannie's subtle clues into a general set of concerns about the environment. In order to clear a space in herself to hear Fannie, Morgan would have had to move aside some of her own tacit assumptions about the land. Perhaps if Morgan had been able to articulate her naturalized relationship (for many of us a *non*relationship) to the land, Fannie might have gained a better understanding of what she needed to articulate, of what tacit beliefs she needed to unpack to convey her thinking about the land.

Listening, Fiumara explains, has nothing to do with a tendency to "assent, consent, or submit" (1990, 183). Authentic listening is nonhegemonic in that it requires, as Heidegger insists, a "dwelling" in another's thought with a part of our mind suspended, recognizing "that we share in both the problem and the solution without being able to escape into neutral and unrelated spaces" (189–90). Authentic listening is experiential. "It is almost as though in order to listen one had to 'become' different, since it is not so much a question of grasping concepts or propositions as of attempting an experience" (191). As DiPardo's study illustrates, without authentic listening, the very programs designed to address social inequality inadvertently reproduce it, "unresolved tensions tugged continually at a fabric of institutional good intentions" (DiPardo 1992, 126).

Discursive regulation is powerful because responses are often automatic. Institutions convince us of what is good, what is natural, what is necessary, and what is right. Authentic listening doesn't occur because the mental categories have already been formed and verified and certified. Morgan knew that being focused matters; she knew what topics she was accustomed to seeing in academic essays. Fannie herself knew the importance of focus and she worked hard to understand Morgan's efforts. But I doubt if either Fannie or Morgan could articulate the differences in cultural and linguistic experience that contributed to Fannie's "writing block."

To imagine a training program that would provide Morgan (and all of us who identify with her) the encouragement, support, and scaffolding to "listen more" we need to understand the psychological processes by which we internalize social norms. To resist social regulation, we need to be aware that our socialization into language and discourse is prompted by anxiety reactions. According to Jacques Lacan's story of language development, we arrive in the world as infants in an undifferentiated psychological state, incapable of regarding ourselves as separate from others. Our first recognition of our separateness comes at what Lacan calls the mirror stage. The mirror stage, the moment of recognizing the Self as Other, as at once over there, in the mirror, and also separate from our caregiver, is traumatic. Linda Brodkey summarizes the import of this recognition: "This moment of split or divided consciousness, literally experienced as a trauma . . . motivates the child to learn language, for only language (specifically, personal pronouns) promises to reunify the now divided self—as an 'I'" (1992, 302). I remember years ago trying to distract my fussy infant daughter by holding her in front of the bathroom mirror. At first the baby in the mirror made her smile, but as soon as she recognized herself as the baby, she turned stubbornly away, crying harder than before and reaching for the doorway.

According to Lacan, the unity offered by language is paradoxically both illusory and necessary. We become anxious when we recognize our split and divided consciousness, and we assume a position within discourse to "heal" the anxiety. We operate more confidently in a discourse or field of power when we align ourselves with one position (an "us" or a "them"). Morgan's confidence seems to depend on her alliance with educational discourse rather than on her effectiveness with Fannie. Until Morgan and the rest of us learn to remain anxious long enough to imagine different ways of responding, we will continue to assume the institutionally constructed discursive position.

Louis Althusser (1971) adds another complication. Through language we not only find relief from the instability of our divided selves, but also inherit a view of the world, an ideology. According to Althusser, institutions "interpellate" us by hailing or calling us in flattering ways, offering us discursively constructed subject positions like the *helpful teacher* or the *responsible writing center tutor* or the *good student*. Because disunity, incoherence, and fragmentation are unpleasant conditions, our desire for unity, rooted in anxiety, makes us susceptible to what Althusser calls ideological interpellation. Many teachers, students, and writing center tutors respond to institutional hailing by readily assuming the positions constructed by the institution. Because we see others in the institution respond in similar fashion to interpellation and because we are rewarded for assuming certain positions, we come to accept this process as normal—even good. We even believe we have freely chosen the positions offered to us. Thus, we become, as the theorists say, the constructed effects of discourse. The discursive practices of the institution "produce" us; we assume, often with a bit of self-righteousness, the positions named and created by the institution. Unwittingly or not, we become both subjects of and subject to educational discourse.

Michel Foucault observes that many people would like to find themselves "on the other side of discourse":

> Inclination speaks out: "I don't want to have to enter this risky world of discourse; I want nothing to do with it insofar as it is decisive and final; I would like to feel it all around me, calm and transparent, profound, infinitely open, with others responding to my expectations, and truth emerging, one by one. All I want is to allow myself to be borne along, within it, and by it, a happy wreck." Institutions reply: "But you have nothing to fear from launching out; we're here to show you dis-

> course is within the established order of things, that we've been wait-
> ing a long time for its arrival, that a place has been set aside for it. . . ."
> (1972, 215–16)

Anxiety is provoked on all sides—by concern about what discourse is,
by fear that we are destined for oblivion without a position within discourse, by awareness of the dangers and the conflicts that lie behind
words. Pretending that we are on "the other side of discourse" in the
writing center or affirming that we are doing the right thing by justify-
ing our practices according to the way things are "in the real world" are
only ways of denying the psychic effects of social regulation. To imagine writing center interactions that do not simply reproduce the status
quo, I turn to postmodern theories of subjectivity.

Reimagining Subjectivity (and Agency) in Composition

Postmodern theorizing has undermined many assumptions about the
individual as autonomous, rational, and existing as an agent in opposition to regulation. Agency is dependent on culture; we cannot hope for
some bizarre escape from social regulation. In *The Psychic Life of Power*,
for example, Judith Butler writes, "Ambivalence is at the heart of
agency" (1997, 18). We can negotiate with the process of discursive
regulation if we stay in anxiety long enough to consider options for responding. Berlin, for example, recognized the way he was being hailed
by his teacher's assignment, and decided to give the teacher what he
was asking for. In a situation like the one Berlin describes, a student
might also call attention to the script he was offered in the assignment
and announce his intention to depart from it. According to Butler, the
subject "deriv[es] its agency from precisely the power it opposes, as
awkward and embarrassing as such a formulation might be, especially
for those who believe that complicity and ambivalence could be rooted
out once and for all" (17). Butler insists "there is no self that is prior to
the convergence or who maintains 'integrity' prior to its entrance into
this conflicted cultural field. There is only the taking up the tools where
they lie, where the very taking up is enabled by the tool lying there"
(1990, 145). Agency is fundamentally rooted in paradox. It is our very
dependence on a discourse that "we never chose" that "paradoxically
initiates and sustains our agency" (1997, 2).

Modernists may operate according to right principles or some
essentialist notion of who we are and "how things are supposed to be"
in institutions, but postmodernists offer a fluid conception of identity,
one that acknowledges the social processes of subjectivity, the ways we

are interpellated, regulated, and motivated by conscious as well as unconscious needs. As Butler explains, discursive power presses us into subordination because it "assumes a psychic form that constitutes the subject's self-identity" (3). Butler illustrates the way cultural fields are regulated by binary frameworks that reward or punish certain performances. She focuses in particular on the cultural field of gender identity. As noticeably gendered people, she says, we are required to imitate certain performances. If we don't, we get "in trouble." Because gender is an imitative performance regulated by compulsive repetition, Butler sees possibilities for agency resulting from the inevitable failures to repeat. She recommends focusing on redescribing these moments that were previously considered unintelligible. For Butler, agency is a matter of revealing the discontinuities that were previously concealed. Composition, like gender identity, requires that students engage repeatedly in a regulated performance of a required subjectivity. To apply Butler's performative notion of agency, writing center workers need to be able to redescribe what appear to be failed performances, and for this to happen, they will first need awareness of the ways they have internalized social norms.

Butler insists on the inescapable and ambivalent psychic effects of social power. "The power imposed upon one is the power that animates one's emergence, and there appears to be no escaping this ambivalence" (198). Butler emphasizes the need to "affirm complicity" as a basis of political agency (29). In "Professing Multiculturalism," composition theorist Min-Zhan Lu asserts a similar theme when she observes, "appropriately mobilized, a sense of ambivalence might be put to constructive uses in writing" (1994, 448). Rather than pretending that discursive regulation doesn't happen or that white middle-class cultural norms are simply the most normal and productive way of doing things, a better way to address social regulation is to mobilize the ambivalence that it generates. To do this, we need a more fluid understanding of subjectivity, one that allows us not only to account for our differences but also to reorganize ourselves in relationship to others, thus avoiding the problem of insisting that we have only one essential self to which we must at all times be true.

As a replacement for the modernist account of the freely choosing, knowable, and autonomous self, I rely on Jane Flax's theorizing of subjectivity. Flax is a professor of political science at Howard University and a practicing psychotherapist. Her work appeals to me for two reasons. For one, she weaves together three strands of theorizing (feminist, postmodern, and psychoanalytic), alternately allowing one strand to compensate for the weakness of the other. For another, she grounds her analysis in considerations of her practice as a therapist and in her triple minority status (white, Jewish, and female) at Howard, a historically black college where she has taught since 1978 (1993, 22). As a therapist, Flax knows how easy it is to collude with dominant beliefs, even when those beliefs harm her clients. Dominant beliefs, she observes, impede our ability to accept randomness, contingency, and the paradoxical effects of our own psychic processes. I agree with Flax's argument that the ability to listen in ways that do not simply reproduce relations of domination is dependent on our ability to regard ourselves as Other. Those of us who are white and middle class need to recognize that we, too, are raced, gendered, and classed subjects rather than just "normal" people.

In theorizing her understanding of subjectivity as multiple, fluid, process-oriented, and yet capable of coherence, Flax rejects two extreme accounts of subjectivity—the modernist unified self and the postmodernist fragmented self. She uses two categories of dysfunctional self-organization—the schizoid and the borderline personality—to illustrate the problems with these two extreme alternatives. At one extreme is the dysfunctional schizoid form of subjectivity, which Flax notes is "an exaggeration of a kind of subjectivity currently valued in the West." Flax regards the common modernist notion of the Cartesian unitary self as "unnecessary, impossible, and a dangerous illusion." She comments, "In the process of therapy, in relations with others, and in political life we encounter many difficulties when subjectivity becomes subject to one normative standard, solidifies into rigid structures, or lacks the capacity to flow readily between different aspects of itself" (93).

Because the thoughts and feelings of a person with schizophrenia are isolated and separated from each other, he or she cannot moderate childish ways of understanding the world with adult ones. Inadvertently, in order to conform to the regulation of a particular kind of subjectivity in their composition classes, students like Hajj, Rebecca, Joe, Nancy, Fannie, and Morgan are expected to separate their lived experiences from the roles they assume in institutions. If they succeed in this split, they can then present a unified position in their papers. This illusion of the unitary self, according to Flax, is an effect of relations of domination. "It can only sustain its unity by splitting off or repressing other parts of its own and others' subjectivity" (109). By splitting off contradictory experiences, the subject "can adapt behavior to achieve predetermined ends while appearing to be an authentic person who is also genuinely concerned for the welfare of others." Flax wryly observes that "the capacity to split reason and feeling, attachment and destruction is highly useful in certain occupations, for example, managing large corporations, designing 'smart bombs,' or defending dangerous chemical plants" (102). We can see this split occurring in Morgan's ability to separate her ethnic and racial ambivalence from her attempts to intervene in Fannie's literacy efforts. We can also see Joe learning to separate his lived experience from his academic performance in order write a paper about animal rights activists without revealing his "bias" as the son and grandson of mink farmers.

Flax contrasts the extreme form of schizoid subjectivity with the other extreme, borderline subjectivity. The person suffering from borderline fragmentation is in such a fragmented and inconstant state that he or she cannot create meaning or move into action. While this form of fragmented subjectivity is sometimes celebrated by postmodernists, Flax reminds us that people who truly cannot sustain some sort of internal coherence slide into "the endless terror, emptiness, desolate loneliness, and fear of annihilation that pervade borderline subjectivity" (103). The borderline person's affective states are so fragmented that he or she lives in constant "emotional vertigo" with a "profound sense of loneliness and emptiness" (105).

According to Flax, both of the extreme forms of subjectivity hold one thing in common: "Neither can experience *simultaneously* the *distinctiveness* of different aspects of subjectivity and their *mutuality*" (italics in orginal) (103). Between the unhealthy and dysfunctional extremes, Flax defines a third, more positive form of subjectivity. She advocates a conception of a decentered, fluid subjectivity, one that avoids false unity but is not a fragmented subjectivity. She theorizes a fluid, multiple, weblike subjectivity capable of being organized for one action and reorganized for another, formed and reformed by familial, political, gendered, somatic, unconscious, and conscious processes, a subjectivity capable of a "less grandiose view of the extent of one's own powers and a more workable sense of responsibility," capable of detaching and distancing from affective experience enough to "enter empathically into the experiences of others or to respect their differences" (106). Flax comments that the task of therapy (and, I would suggest, composition teaching and tutoring) is not "the discovery (or construction) of a solid, unitary, pristine, and undistorted self lying somewhere deep down inside" but rather the development of multiple ways of organizing subjectivity (107).

Flax insists that a multiple and fluid conception of subjectivity is essential for a time when recognition of differences is the most pressing political problem. She observes "Since discussions about justice implicitly or explicitly assume and generate assumptions about who 'we' are and why we are living together, discourse about justice cannot do without concepts of subjectivity" (111). The same holds true for understanding writing in the contact zone. A postmodern notion of justice, which Flax conceives of as a process rather than a set of rules and principles, is dependent on the construction of transitional spaces, spaces that depend on our ability to be fluid, multiple subjects. To explain her concept of transitional space, Flax relies on the work of D.W. Winnicott and other object relations psychoanalysts who stress the importance of relations with others in the constitution of identity. Using Winnicott, Flax explains that humans live simultaneously in three realities: inner, external, and transitional. If we are healthy, the transitional space is a space of play and creative transformation, a place that grows in richness throughout life, not one we discard as adults. Transitional space is where we deal with the loss of omnipotence, with the pressures of the outer world, and with the conflicts of the inner world. It is a space that can emerge only with "neither too much nor too little impingement from either the inner or outer world" (121). In transitional space, we engage in symbolization, creatively transforming culture. Because we are never free of the conflict between inner and outer realities, transitional spaces are part of the lifelong process of reconciling self and other.

Flax links her understanding of justice to the concept of transitional space. Otherwise, justice would be submission to the regulation of the outer world, a submission to anxiety. "Transitional spaces serve as defenses against the fear of multiplicity, ambivalence, and uncertainty. This fear often tempts us to try to collapse all our worlds into one . . . [rather than] challenge or play with the limits or restrictions required by the outer world" (122–23). Flax identifies four characteristics of a playful and creative transitional space that I will use to reconsider the work between Fannie and Morgan and to imagine other directions their work might have taken: reconciliation, reciprocity, recognition, and judgment.

Reconciliation. According to Flax, justice "requires a unity of differences," not a unity based on a uniform standard, but a "new multiple unity" based on mutuality and "incorporation" rather than "annihilation of opposites and distinctions" (123–24). To reconcile differences, we need "to extend or preserve the play of difference." If Fannie and Morgan thought of themselves as working in a transitional space, one where they were supposed to extend the play of differences rather than conform to a mainstream standard, they might have spent more time talking about the life experiences they bring to writing at the university: the languages, the cultures, and the personal history of schooling that has shaped their identities. They might creatively imagine what an essay would be like if it incorporated these diverse histories. They might imagine ways of writing to convey these imaginings. These possibilities may sound intrusive, time-consuming, wasteful, and perhaps even ridiculous—a sure sign that we expect students to split the inner reality of the self from the outer reality of school culture. Carol Severino has observed that when we imagine the student moving from home culture to school culture, "the assumption is that after the student, with the help of the guide, crosses the bridge, s/he burns it" (1992, 8). Unfortunately, as Severino observes, "usually, when we speak of crossing boundaries, it is the student who is on the journey, not the teacher, and the implication is that the student has only a one-way ticket" (8). What if instead, as Severino suggests, we imagine the bridge a means for student and tutor to move back and forth between cultures?

Tutorials could instead focus on the often noncontiguous worlds of public and private life and on the means of negotiating between the inner and outer realities of our multiple selves. Can we expect eighteen- or nineteen-year-old college students to generate these discussions? Well, we now expect them to pretend the gaps between home and school don't exist, so inviting them to discuss the gaps is a more potent gesture. Can we expect Fannie to have the vocabulary, the self-awareness, the self-confidence to carry this conversation? No, not initially. But we can expect it of Morgan if, during her training to become a tutor and a high school English teacher, we give her opportunities to practice thinking of herself as a raced, gendered, classed, multiply situated self. Because of her race, Morgan may have had more practice thinking about her multiple and fluid subjectivity than have many white middle-class tutors. The white middle-class tutors (and their directors) will be more challenged to recognize themselves as raced, classed, and gendered rather than simply as "normal" humans. By developing and demonstrating awareness of the formation and reformation of their identity, writing center tutors, no matter how awkwardly they do this, can encourage the creation of transitional space where they can play with and challenge cultural expectations, reimagining social futures.

Reciprocity. According to Flax, reciprocity "connotes a continuous though imprecisely defined sharing of authority and mutuality of decision." Transitional spaces characterized by reciprocity "press us to resist false accommodation to ill-fitting demands." The practice of reciprocity does not require equality of power, only resistance to domination, which occurs whenever normative practices or objective standards intrude into transitional space. In theory, reciprocity should characterize writing center interactions, but the regulatory nature of composition inevitably pushes tutorial sessions toward objective standards and normative practices. Morgan, for example, "never really surrendered control; somehow, the message always came across that Morgan knew more than Fannie about the ideas at hand" (DiPardo 1992, 138). Yet, DiPardo also observes, "As [Morgan] struggled to come to terms with her own ethnic ambivalence, to defend herself against a vociferous chorus proclaiming her 'not black enough,' Morgan had reason to take heart in Fannie's dramatic and rather trying process of transition," particularly since Fannie was "learning to inhabit both arenas" (141). To create transitional space in writing centers, training programs would not mirror the outer reality of "objective" or "normative" standards but rather hold those in tension with inner realities, sustaining transitional space to imagine possibilities for transformation.

Nancy Welch's "excess-ive theory of revision" is based on this understanding of reciprocity. She asks, "what will happen when we begin to read, write, and teach at that tense, problematic, and fascinating boundary between *individual* and *society*—reading, writing, and teaching with an excess-ive and pluralized understanding of these terms and of the intricate braids that make it impossible for us to distinguish between the two?" (1997, 167). To revise a culture or a paper, one must move beyond an either/or choice between repudiation of or identification with the culture of power. Tutoring, as Aaron Schutz and Anne Ruggles Gere (1998) argue, must also move beyond caring for the private and the individual into a reciprocal understanding of the relationship between social forces and individual "problems."

Recognition. Flax identifies the challenge of "acknowledging the legitimacy of others" (1993, 124), accepting their differences while at the same time identifying with them. We must recognize ourselves as both separate from and connected to the Other, experiencing our separation "as other than abandonment or domination" (125). Without this ability to recognize the legitimacy of others, we cannot imagine ways to remake our relationships with authorities, with rules. Morgan, like many tutors, struggled with her frustration at Fannie's silence. DiPardo quotes an end-of-term interview in which Morgan described her lasting impression of Fannie.

> "I just remember her sitting there," Morgan recalled, "and talking to her, and it's like, 'well I don't know, I don't know' . . . Fannie just has so many doubts, and she's such a hesitant person, she's so withdrawn, and mellow, and quiet. . . . A lot of times, she'd just say, 'well I don't know what I'm supposed to write. . . . Well, I don't like this, I don't like my writing'." (133)

Understandably but regrettably, Morgan's sense of her effectiveness is defined by Fannie's responses. "Are you learnin' anything from me?" she'd ask. Morgan's training gave her expertise, strategies, and methods, but it did not encourage her to separate her need to perform well from Fannie's reluctant response. It did not teach her to be curious about Fannie's reluctance. Instead, she was frustrated by Fannie's failure to benefit from her helpful intentions. Rather than recognize

Fannie as distinct, rather than risk identifying with Fannie's voiceless-ness, Morgan attempted to extend discursive regulation, to fix Fannie's writing problems by trying to make her conform.

Judgment. Flax defines judgment as a process—not as the applica-tion of an external reality but as "balancing and proportion" (125). Judgment calls not only on logic and objectivity but also on empathy and imagination. Judgment involves movement between evidence and reflection, Self and Other, individual and collective, past and fu-ture (125). Judgment requires us to move back and forth between mul-tiple realities, it "encourage[s] us to tolerate ambiguity and ambiva-lence without losing a sense of individual location and responsibility" (125). Morgan could not see, play with, tolerate, appreciate, or imagine Fannie's point of view because she saw it from the point of view of the university, the institution—from the universal gaze of regulation. From this perspective, the problem appears to reside in Fannie; Fannie needs to remake herself.

Readers may wonder just how fair it is to expect so much from a writing center, and from tutors who are undergraduates themselves. When I first read DiPardo's essay, my reaction was similar. I felt uneasy when I recognized in Morgan some of my own reactions to nonmain-stream students, and I translated that into thinking how unfair it was to expect more of her, given her position in the institution and all of the constraints operating on that position. Yet I think DiPardo was right to shine the light on Morgan because it is Morgan and others like her who work on the front lines with nonmainstream students. We have trans-ferred responsibility to them, and we are responsible for the programs that recruit and train them and for the budgets that support that im-portant work. But Morgan, like many undergraduate tutors, had only a few hours of training and received little supervision. DiPardo con-cludes her essay by challenging those responsible for such programs to think more realistically about the kinds of support and guidance that new tutors and teachers need, particularly "the need to monitor one's ethnocentric biases and faulty assumptions" (1992, 142).

A training program that creates an identity crisis for white middle-class students and teachers by inviting them to scrutinize their entitle-ments and denaturalize their merits will certainly generate resistance. Flax consistently confronts resistance from women's studies scholars for her use of postmodern theory. Postmodernism destabilizes the con-ceptual grounds on which many intellectual pursuits and programs are based. Flax observes, "If one takes some of its central ideas seriously, even while resisting or rejecting others, postmodernism is bound to in-duce a profound uneasiness, or threatened identity, especially among white Western intellectuals. Our consciousness and positions are among its primary subjects of critical analysis" (1993, 133). Within postmodernism "there is no trump available that we can rely on to solve all disputes" (138), "no transcendental standpoint or mind unencumbered by its own language and stories" (139), and no "neutral rules that could provide certain guarantees" (145). The redesign of the academic identity kit relies on the ability of the designers to remake themselves, to imagine themselves as multiple fluid subjects.

Will my suggestions for rethinking writing center practice result in complete anarchy? Will institutions withdraw funding from writing centers because they are not doing what they are supposed to be doing? I don't think so. I am not recommending that tutors tell students to repudiate all routine practices and authority. Rather, I am recommending that they tell students how these authoritative practices work without automatically and unconsciously endorsing them. I am recommending that they de-naturalize the practices so that students can make decisions about the extent to which they want to conform to the design, to acknowledge the norm encoded in the design, and even depart from it or create a new design. Flax reminds us "without pregiven structures and systems of signification, no creativity would be possible. On the other hand, the individual can creatively transform what is given, including language, texts, and games of various sorts, in part by bringing something of inner reality into the process" (121). To cultivate the arts of the contact zone, to coax people out of their safe houses into a mediation of differences, we need to first cultivate the psychic space for negotiation to occur. This is not as simple as developing new tutoring strategies or a new code of ethical principles; rather, it is as difficult as regarding ourselves as Other. It requires a willingness to scrutinize our role and responsibility as change agents within the institution. When we learn to do this with some degree of facility, students may decide, in some cases, to match our expectations; in other cases, they will teach us how to redesign our social futures. In the meantime, we can thank them for breaking the flattering mirror of mainstream assumptions and for creating opportunities for us to transform our selves and our practices.

Notes

1. An early version of this paper was presented at a 1998 on-line CCCC session organized by Marilyn Cooper. I am grateful to Marilyn, the on-line respondents, and especially Carol Severino, whose comments helped me rethink and refine my argument.

2. Ogbu defines involuntary minorities in contrast to autonomous minorities (e.g., Jews or Mormons) and immigrant minorities. Involuntary minorities are "people who were originally brought into the United States society involuntarily through slavery, conquest, or colonization. Thereafter, they were relegated to menial positions and denied true assimilation into the mainstream. American Indians, black Americans, Mexican Americans, and native Hawaiians are examples" (1987, 153).

Chapter Four

Getting Unstuck
Rearticulating the Nodal Points [1]

It may be asked, when a large, well-organized opponent is about to come to you, how do you deal with it? The answer is that you first take away what they like, and then they will listen to you.
—Sun Tzu, *The Art of War*

Of the many stories shared among writing center people, the ones about the relationships with faculty resonate with familiar themes—faculty suspicion about the writing center, refusal to grant departmental voting rights to writing center professional staff, faculty dismay about the condition of papers that "went through" the writing center (as though the writing center were a laundry service), exploitation of part-timers, confusion about the status/role of writing center directors. Not long ago, a writing center friend told about coming up behind a group of colleagues gathered around a bulletin board. From a distance she could see her name on the recently posted list of nominations for the Outstanding Teacher award. Next to her name, someone had drawn several large question marks. As she drew nearer to the group, she overheard her colleagues question her eligibility. In their minds—even though she had recently earned tenure and regularly taught courses for graduate and undergraduate students—the fact that she also worked with students in the writing center placed her outside the group of teachers eligible for awards.

81

Writing center people often gravitate toward practical solutions to these ongoing problems. They urge one another to get control of their budgets and get out from under the English department. They advise one another to make the writing center indispensable by matching its philosophy to the university's five-year plan. These practical solutions solve practical problems, but they don't change undervalued service positions. Writing centers are marked by the same traditional notions of what women provide—refuge, nurturance, emotional support, personal guidance—qualities that generally are not integrated theoretically or structurally into the teaching or research mission of the university.[2] Writing centers are expected to be the handmaidens of autonomous literacy—a value-free, culturally neutral notion of literacy—which although extensively challenged theoretically is still strongly at work in the academy. Universities expect writing centers to deal with heterogeneity—students who speak English as a second language, students who use a nondominant dialect, students who have learning disabilities, students who don't follow assignment guidelines, students from cultural and economic backgrounds not accounted for in the middle-class assumptions of schooling—by controlling it (or cleaning it up) rather than by interpreting or negotiating it.

Even though the practical solutions do not always address the frustration caused by being denied social recognition, faculty status, and voting rights, many writing center workers keep silent rather than create new battlefronts and call negative attention to the writing center. In spite of their precarious political position, writing center workers are often warmed by the good feelings they derive from their work. They believe in the power of ideas and the importance of communication, and they hope that what they do in the writing center provides students with access to that communicative power. They derive satisfaction not from large salaries or institutional recognition, but from the feeling that they are doing the right thing—that they are helping others. They like to imagine writing center work as an effort to make the world more perfect. Now I've come along with this book and undermined those good feelings.

In this chapter, I want to offer alternatives to a position stuck in silent frustration not simply because I want to enhance the administrative positioning of writing centers (although that would be a happy side effect) but rather because I do not believe students are well served by a writing center that neutralizes differences. I believe that writing centers can work more effectively with students if that work is situated within the contrasting democratic desire to understand and negotiate difference rather than the institutional need to manage or eliminate it. Literacy work within a pluralistic democracy is deeply paradoxical. The ability of a writing center to move differently within this paradox is dependent on a better understanding of how literacy and power operate within a democratic system.

Positioning writing centers to contribute to a dialogue about difference within higher education is not a simple reversal of hierarchy—a move out of a subordinate service position. Such repositioning demands a much more complicated, ongoing effort to address the conflicts embedded in the literacy myth without expecting a tidy resolution. Even though revisionist literacy theorists have challenged us to see that factors of race, ethnicity, gender, and class, not literacy skills, are more likely to determine the degree of participation in the mainstream, the work of the writing center is still implicated in the myth of meritocracy underlying literacy teaching, the idea that success goes to all those who work to earn it. To rearticulate the work of the writing center in ways that avoid its implication in meritocratic myths about literacy, I offer theoretical arguments about the nature of language and power from theorists such as Vygotsky and Laclau and Mouffe. However, academic theorizing alone will not address the problematic position of writing centers within institutions. To move writing centers out of reactive into proactive positions, I apply some practical wisdom about rebuilding relationships from Harriet Goldhor Lerner's trilogy— *The Dance of Anger* (1985), *The Dance of Intimacy* (1989), and *The Dance of Deception* (1993). Lerner's work is based in family systems theory, which recognizes the complex interconnections of culture and behavior patterns, particularly the ways that unprocessed events create "sticky" issues in systems and keep individuals stuck in unproductive behaviors. While academic theorizing is useful for analyzing the operations of language and power that maintain existing relationships, this self-help discourse suggests steps we might take to change unhealthy patterns in relationships.

Some readers may believe that on *their* campus any threat to the literacy myth would meet with immediate disapproval or that as people in low-status positions, they cannot question the status quo. I don't believe writing centers have to wait for institutions to change. This chapter suggests steps that writing centers can take to theoretically integrate their work into the teaching and research mission of higher education. By articulating academic theory and the popular discourse on relationships, I foreground my conviction that change in the operations of the academic community, particularly its tacit habits of exclusion, must begin with the network of relationships we build—or more often fail to build—in our workplaces.[3]

I hope that my carnivalesque juxtaposition of self-help theory with academic theory will offer generative insights, because the relationship issues we negotiate in daily life are often replicated in our institutional lives. As Lerner observes, "the patterns that keep us stuck in our close relationships derive their shape and form from the patterns of a stuck society" (1985, 223). Her use of a dance metaphor throughout her three books calls attention to the cultural rhythms that keep us in self-defeating and problem-perpetuating behaviors. The metaphor also reminds us what to expect if we change the pattern: there will be counter-moves and demands from our "dance" partners to get back in step. To facilitate change in writing center positioning, I will explore the potential of three crucial moves suggested by family systems therapy: Reconnecting with historical issues; defining a new position; and moving differently. I believe that by reengaging with the history of remediation and redefining themselves theoretically, writing center workers can develop effective political strategies that will move institutions toward more democratic literacy practices.

Reconnecting with Sticky Issues

History isn't dry; it's sticky, it can get all over your hands.
—Margaret Atwood, *The Robber Bride*

A frequent starting point for improving relationships is what family systems therapists call family-of-origin work, a self-examination that seeks to understand relationships from our past, particularly the relationships of our formative years. Dysfunctional patterns from those relations can influence our reactions to current relationships. Therapists often say that until we are aware of the repressed issues from the past, we often continue to set ourselves up to repeat patterns, believing subconsciously that with one more go-round we might get things to turn out right. This pathological repetition keeps us locked in position and prevents change.

Change in writing center positioning is similarly blocked by the sticky history of remediation that haunts writing center work. In the late 1970s and early 1980s, institutions distanced themselves from literacy markers of race, class, and ethnicity by establishing writing centers to manage the differences. Anne DiPardo and Mike Rose have called attention to the ongoing institutional ambivalence about meeting the needs of underrepresented students. DiPardo argues that faculty remain "essentially unchanged" because tutoring programs are separated from the essential business of the university; "remedial" students are often taught by adjunct or part-time faculty (1993, 172). Moreover, as DiPardo points out, when budgets are constrained, no one acknowledges the socioeconomic conditions of the students; instead they blame them for not already being prepared for college. Mike Rose connects the ambivalence about students' needs with a conservative force in higher education. He claims that "the American university has yet to figure out, conceptually or institutionally, how to integrate its general education mission with its research mission" (1989, 197).

Our cultural programming has set us up to respond in patterned ways, creating rewards and punishments for certain performances, making it difficult to give up historical beliefs and behaviors. Regarding marriages that suffer from a lack of intimate communication, Lerner makes the point that "as long as women function *for* men, men have no need to change" (1989, 8). The same is true in the relationship between writing centers and the university. As long as writing centers enable students to get through the system, the system has no reason to change. Conforming to the system and seeking approval from it does not result in improved relationships or improved practices. To move differently, however, creates anxiety because writing centers are supposed to manage rather than foreground departures from culturally accepted norms. They are supposed to make do with what they have, to keep the home tidy, and put a perky ribbon in their hair when visitors come. Moreover, literacy is a highly reactive historical issue because of its complicated connections to other social myths.

To distance themselves from this historical issue, many writing centers figuratively scraped a remedial connotation off their hands and aligned themselves with the process movement in composition studies where they found a neutral vocabulary for describing their work— "collaborative" and "student-centered." The rush to integrate the latest computer technology provided another rationale for writing center work. Gradually, students themselves found how valuable it was to talk with a friendly writing center tutor, and eventually the services of most writing centers had expanded far beyond a remedial focus.

However, because history, as Atwood says, is sticky, writing centers are vulnerable in times of shifting budgets and changing administrations, and this vulnerability can position them as eager-to-please wives, ready to serve the needs of faculty, whatever they may be. Even though writing centers have sought to put remedial history behind them and to be viewed as essential resources for all writers, the therapists would say they are still driven by historical forces; unresolved issues from the past continue to lurk beneath the surface. As places historically intended to preserve the status quo by shaping students to suit the system, writing centers experience anxiety if they begin to probe the contradictions of practice. Why, for example, are writing center tutors *not* supposed to write anything on students' papers when these students' teachers *are* supposed to write on them? Why are students exhorted to choose their own topics, then sometimes told that their topics are not appropriate? Why are students told to write about their personal experiences but expected to use academic diction and genres? Why do some instructors tell students not to bother with the writing center, to do their *own* work instead?

Even though many writing centers have put their remedial history behind them, the writing center questions that won't go away—questions about the ethics of collaboration, about relationships with faculty, about proofreading, about dependency, about what to call the people who work in writing centers—are all rooted in the historical fact that writing centers were expected to solve the problems students weren't supposed to have when they come to college. Rather than study the contradictions of practice, writing centers have avoided them by exhorting tutors not to write on papers and not to question teachers or assignments. Through these avoidance patterns writing centers inadvertently contribute to distancing mechanisms that prevent cultural change. If writing centers were instead to come to terms with their history of remediation, they could generate an understanding of the economic, cultural, and political forces that come into conflict with the tacit expectations of academic culture and inhibit literacy learning.

A therapeutic reexamination of the past closely resembles what many political theorists call *critical reflection*. Antonio Gramsci (1971), for example, writes about the process of understanding ourselves as part of an historical process. Frederic Jameson argues for the need for developing cognitive maps that provide a "heightened sense" of our "positioning as individual and collective subjects" (1992, 54). Michel Foucault begins his political analysis with genealogy, emphasizing the value of understanding the ancestry of systems and ideas. As places originally designed to handle the students whose literacy backgrounds departed from white middle-class expectations, writing centers represent what Foucault would call the response of a disciplined society. Instead of excluding underprepared students from the university, we used, in Foucault's words, "procedures of individualization to mark exclusion" (1979, 199). Many writing labs were supposed to correct, measure, and supervise abnormal writers to help them meet the standards set by the institution. In Foucault's analysis of the ways that systems make subjects out of people, "pastoral power" is one of the most effective. Pastoral power aims for individual salvation, is self-sacrificial, looks after individuals, and is exercised by knowing the inside of people's minds. Its power seeks to shape individuals into very specific patterns and forms (1982, 213–14). Elements of pastoral power lurk in the history and the training programs of many writing centers. On most campuses, writing centers continue to focus on changing individuals to fit into systems because the general education and research missions haven't changed. Conforming to and seeking approval from the system does not result in improved relationships or improved literacy practices.

To contribute to revisions of curriculum, rather than to the mere reinforcement of curriculum, writing centers need to reconnect with the population of students designated on any particular campus as remedial and to work with this population to foreground the class, cultural, and racial issues submerged in autonomous literacy. This autonomous view of literacy, according to Gunther Kress, has treated individuals as *users* of an existing system rather than as potential transformers or remakers of it (1997, 114). One of the major conceptual stumbling blocks to reconnecting with a "remedial" population is the "community" metaphor that has created a false veneer for much of the work in composition and writing centers. The academic community metaphor encourages writing center workers to imagine their work as welcoming and initiating and disguises its truer, disciplining function. Writing center workers perceive students classified as remedial as individuals needing their help rather than as potential research partners.

Even though literacy researchers have demonstrated that language is a site of cultural conflict and that we often use language for exclusionary rather than inclusionary purposes, writing center workers theorize their work as enabling students to understand and enter the academic community. Even though conflicts among different communities' literacy practices are visible in writing centers, even though writing centers were established to meet the needs of students who were raised in communities quite different from the academic community, the community metaphor has suppressed discussion of the conflicts some students encounter in their efforts to join the academic community. As Patricia Bizzell observes, the invocation of community allows us at once to promise not to exclude anyone and at the same time not to admit anyone "truly disruptive of the status quo" (1991, 59). Bizzell argues that composition studies' invocation of community functions as "an utterance that helps middle-class teachers fend off criticism from those both above and below them in the social order." As she puts it, "The very warmth of the word conceals the fact that the academic neighborhood does not welcome everyone equally. Just as in other communities, tacit exclusions obtain" (59). Fortunately, composition scholars like Bizzell, Joseph Harris, Marilyn Cooper, and others have been chipping away at the community veneer. They point out that the term *community* offers little acknowledgment of or regard for communities other than the academic one, and it entertains little openness to flux and change within that community. By relinquishing the neutrality of the academic community metaphor, we are more likely to recognize the price some students must pay in their attempts to join this community and more likely to acknowledge the invisible roadblocks to membership. Outside the protection of the community metaphor, writing center workers can also talk more frankly with students about what is lost and what is gained as we move among communities.

I have argued in this section for the value of reconnecting with a remedial history not because I believe this is the only role of writing centers but rather because efforts to distance from it have created hot spots and ignored the cultural work of literacy. Joyce Kinkead has observed that little has been written about the politics of writing centers, the issues of cultural and linguistic diversity, or the potential of the writing center as a site of research (Kinkead and Harris 1993, 246–47). Because of the academy's ambivalence about underrepresented students, much of the writing center's potential as a research site has been untapped. To transform writing centers into "hothouse[s] of knowledge-making" (Spooner 1993, 3), writing center workers need to address the hot issues of the past. Writing centers have often prided themselves on their tradition of responding to local conditions, which is a healthy behavior as long as it is done out of a sense of self-differentiation and direction. But when response to local conditions develops from an anxious reactivity related to unprocessed issues of the past, we repeat patterns rather than change orientation. Engaging with the sticky history of remediation in positive ways that emphasize the value of understanding difference, rather than reacting to it, can position writing centers to achieve their potential as rich sites of research. If writing centers no longer fall back on the protection of a community metaphor or an autonomous model of literacy, they will be in a better position to study and reflect upon the conflicts that students negotiate as they learn to write in the academy. Thus, they will be more clearly involved in research and teaching. Working within a social action model of research that involves students as participants, writing centers will be less connected with the need to serve and to please and more connected with the desire to understand, to articulate, and to interpret.

Defining a New Position

The most important principle underlying family systems theory is that the renegotiation of roles must begin with an increased self-focus rather than a reactive focus on the Other. Lerner argues that *"change occurs only as we begin thinking about and working on the self—rather than staying focused on and reactive to the other"* (italics in original) (1989, 86). For too long writing centers have been triangulated in the relationship between teachers and students to manage cultural anxiety about literacy. Family systems theory recognizes that humans are inevitably involved in triangular relationships. As Lerner puts it, "Triangles solve a problem by lowering anxiety when it can no longer be contained between two persons" (148–49). Because triangles are inevitable in human systems, the key to healthy functioning is to recognize one's position in a triangle and to take responsible rather than reactive positions in it. We develop political effectiveness by recognizing that we are not completely *deter-*

mined by our relationships even though we may have been culturally programmed to react in order to please others or to conform to their expectations. Writing center workers do not have to respond in ways that others would like them to respond.

To respond differently, Lerner says, people need to "struggle with theory rather than to focus narrowly on technique" (202). To become legitimate academic units rather than service units, writing centers need to undertake an ongoing effort to define their practice theoretically. Listing services offered and counting the numbers of student visits are important administrative tasks, but they do not answer the question of why we need writing centers. The work of Lev Vygotsky offers rich possibilities for theorizing the work of writing centers in ways that go beyond listing services and saying they offer individualized instruction. Such a definition suggests that only certain people need individualized instruction and that intellectual development occurs only in this manner.

Many think of Vygotsky as building on the work of Piaget when in fact he was challenging some Piagetian assumptions. Although interested in Piaget's observations about the stages of intellectual development, Vygotsky wanted to understand the genesis of intellectual development. Through his own empirical work, he found that intellectual development does not occur as a gradual flowering of innate individual ability but that our thinking and language develop as a result of our interactions with others. The notion that intellect develops as a result of interactions with others justifies writing center practice more powerfully than does a list of multiple services provided. But this theoretical justification of intellectual development is at odds with many cherished beliefs of the academy, including the systems we have in place to safeguard "individual" work, such as plagiarism policies, protection of intellectual property, and the Library of Congress classification system, which demands a single author.

In light of the academic reverence for individual production, writing centers need to foreground Vygotsky's strongest conclusion: the intellect develops by *participating* in human relationships, not by sitting on the sidelines and listening to the rules being explained. When Vygotsky sought to understand what made writing difficult, why so many struggle to bring thought into words, he found that writing requires a double abstraction, one from the sound of speech, another from the interlocutor (1988, 182). His point is that we cannot abstract from something that was never there in the first place. Inner speech is not something that is simply there as the result of an individual developmental process. It is formulated through a social process of interacting with others. If we do not have the opportunities to interact with others on topics that we must write about, then we cannot internalize the concepts we must draw on in order to write.

Within a Vygotskian framework, an interactive relationship with someone willing to construct a scaffold for the work of abstraction, someone willing to recognize and engage existing patterns of literacy, is essential for literacy development—not just an extra service for "undeveloped" individuals. This theorizing makes writing centers essential to the pedagogical mission of the university, and it suggests a research mission for the writing center that seeks to understand the desires, needs, interests, interactions, and emotions that impact literacy development. According to Vygotsky, not only do individuals develop language and thought from the outside in, but they also receive motivation through interactions with others. "Thought is not begotten by thought; it is engendered by motivation, i.e., by our desires and needs, our interests and emotions. Behind every thought there is an affective-volitional tendency" (1988, 252).

Vygotsky's shift from a focus on individual performance to a focus on the social, interactive, and relational nature of literacy development is echoed in much literacy research. Shirley Brice Heath (1988) explains that true literacy develops not just from opportunities to read and write but from opportunities to talk about what has been read and written, from participation in literacy events. Good teachers provide these opportunities in classrooms, but too often the floor is controlled by those students already comfortable with academic ways with words. Heath insists that only by *participation* in literacy events does one learn the contextually relevant meta-rules that govern written discourse. Deborah Brandt identifies relationships as the key to literacy development: "People do not read themselves into literacy—they have to be talked into it" (1990, 113). Richard Ohmann also emphasizes the relational aspect of literacy: "Like every other human activity or product, [literacy] embeds social relationships within it . . . Literacy is an exchange between classes, races, the sexes, and so on" (1988, 226).

Theorists who place relationships at the center of literacy development make it clear how difficult it is to achieve these relationships in a classroom. Bizzell stresses "how difficult it can be to make education truly reciprocal, and not something done to one person by another" (1988, 151). Elizabeth Ellsworth comments on the same difficulty:

> Dialogue in its conventional sense is impossible in the culture at large because at this historic moment, power relations between raced, classed, and gendered students and teachers are unjust. The injustice of these relations and the way in which those injustices distort communication cannot be overcome in a classroom, no matter how committed the teacher and students are to overcoming conditions that perpetuate suffering. (1989, 316)

Writing centers are not immune from the distortions in communication that occur because of social conditions. Many of the failures of literacy work occur because those who are thoroughly socialized in the dominant discourse are unaware of the tacit expectations and assumptions that are carried in academic literacy practices. If writing centers are theorized as essential interactive sites of literacy learning, then the need to make the tacit explicit as well as the need to acknowledge different positions with relationship to academic power come into sharp focus. In writing tutorials where underlying political tensions and ambivalence about one's relationship to academe are not addressed, we engage in what Louise Z. Smith calls "feigned patience, feigned effort, feigned teaching, and feigned learning" (1991, 66). According to Smith, rules of politeness make it easier for us to engage in "dissemblances, double-binds, and mystifications" (70) than to frankly address the underlying tensions that interfere with real learning.

With less emphasis on providing tutorial "service" and more theoretical awareness of the tacit work of literacy, writing centers can be places for unpacking the differing assumptions in worldviews and for understanding the role of social relationships in the development of multiple literacies. The intransitive academic tasks students perform to earn grades at the university are embedded in power relations that characterize the student as a "young beginner . . . a presexual, preeconomic, prepolitical person" (Miller 1991, 87). Writing centers can work with students to intervene in these disempowering representations and to find opportunities for students to offer more complicated self-representations. Writing center workers will need to think of themselves as scholars and researchers if they are to going to undertake tasks like these. My capacity, for example, to contribute to committee discussions about students from other countries who have difficulty with the Western tradition of documentation will be strengthened if I am knowledgeable about how other cultures understand intellectual property. My capacity to persuade will not be strong if I simply testify on behalf of the students' difficulty. However, if I can also demonstrate how our own culture's notion of text ownership is being eroded by postmodern theory and technology, I might contribute to pedagogical change. I can't develop this important knowledge if I respond to all institutional requests for services, such as the professor who recently called me to suggest I purchase software that promises to help students assess their study skills. I'll need theoretical evidence to explain convincingly that this technology will not do more to improve study skills than pencil and paper exercises did ten years ago, that it will in fact be a distraction from the real thing—a relationship that motivates learning. I'll need the same kind of evidence to respond to the request that the writing center prepare to teach keyboarding to foreign students during the December holiday break. If writing centers stop overfunctioning as service units, they can put more energy into theorizing about what happens in the center and use that knowledge "to give feedback, to share our perspective, to state clearly our values and beliefs and then stand firmly behind them" (Lerner 1989, 209). A theoretically grounded understanding of the importance of the interactive learning in the writing center can move writing centers into a more clearly defined position, a position integrated with the teaching and research mission of higher education.

Moving Differently

To move out of silence and into dialogue about difference, writing centers need to "share more" of what they learn from the students who reveal the invisible borders to discourse communities, students whose lived experience reveals the contradictions in our democratic discourse about literacy. Creating a climate in which information can be shared requires the courage to move against "patriarchal injunctions that promote silence and denial" (Lerner 1993, 154). Universities, grounded as they are in masculine epistemology and hierarchical top-down decision making and charged with the job of protecting knowledge and safeguarding traditions, are especially resistant to change. Change on the part of the writing center is not something to attempt frivolously. Lerner insists that one moves into dialogue only after a great deal of personal grounding, reflection, and research into historical positioning. Even then one must be prepared to manage the anxiety triggered by the inevitable demands to "change back." A process approach to change eschews aggressive or demanding approaches, which only entrench positions.

We must ground the move into honest dialogue about literacy in an understanding of what is at stake as well as what has prevented the dialogue. When Bizzell argues, "[W]e should complicate our communal relations with one another, share more, reveal more" (1991, 66), she acknowledges that "sharing more" is a dangerous move to make, one that may well expose the "explosive realm of major contradictions in our national life" (1991, 67). To change a worldview, one needs to find and name its contradictions, to locate the places where it leaks. Gramsci (1971) locates the possibilities for change in the contact between individuals of different classes and allegiances. Because writing centers are a site of this contact, they can become significant sites of change. However, Gramsci linked his hopes for social change to a contest between essentialist social categories, such as class divisions. Such a vision of change will not work for writing centers. As marginal as writing center workers often feel, they are part of the institution that provides their paychecks. Moreover, a contestatory practice of change often takes an either/or strategy; if one side wins, the other loses. The defensiveness that occurs in this approach does not lead to mutual understanding or to lasting institutional change.

Writing centers are uniquely situated to begin revealing the contradictions in the dominant representations of undergraduates, but a counterhegemonic stance requires more than personal courage and conviction. It requires persuasive capacity grounded in a workable theory of political change. Lerner cautions that "truth-telling demands far more than 'honesty' and good intentions, as these are conventionally defined. It also requires us to relinquish our habitual, patterned modes of reaction and thought, so that we can move toward an expanded vision of reality that is multilayered, complex, inclusive, and accurate" (1993, 213). Without recognizing how partial, subjective, and contextual our situated "knowing" is, we try to impose a version of our reality on others (209–13). The ability of writing centers to explain their understandings is also limited by the language of power. Because worldviews are linguistically defined, the terms for naming a different reality are not readily available. People who live on the border between realities find it difficult to articulate their understandings. As Mike Rose puts it, "Having crossed boundaries, you sometimes can't articulate what you know, or what you know seems strange" (1989, 241). Not only is our expression limited, but our thinking as well. As Victor Villanueva Jr. observes, hegemony "limits how deeply we look" (1993, 121). In order to overcome the frustration of lacking a language and a vision, I once again make the point that writing centers need to be grounded in critical discourses. Even though this critical language is not easily attained, it confers "new powers of understanding and articulation" (Johnson 1986/87, 43) when it can be applied to concrete cases, which are plentiful in the writing center.

As an alternative to a confrontational approach to change, I propose a political strategy theorized by Ernesto Laclau and Chantal Mouffe in their book *Hegemony & Socialist Strategy* (1985). Laclau and Mouffe argue that the possibility for a deeper democracy exists in an acceptance of the radically open nature of the political terrain, the multiplicity of viewpoints in circulation. They recommend not a contestatory political practice, not a hopeful holdout for a revolutionary event, but an ongoing effort to articulate multiple discourses in the direction of greater democratic practices. Their key term—*articulation*—as used in the United States is associated with clear, carefully enunciated spoken language, but it gains added meaning from its British use. Stuart Hall (1986) explains the nuances of the British meaning of the word with the image of an articulated lorry, a truck linked to other vehicles. This more fully developed sense of articulation includes not only the clear, well-defined expression of a position, but also the productive linkage of that position with other concerns. One needs to clearly articulate a need or position, roam in search of concerns that can be linked to that issue, and move in concert with others to address that need.

Articulation is a political strategy that can work for writing centers. Being prepared to link diverse concerns is rhetorical and persuasive more than it is contentious and oppositional. Articulation is also an appropriately postmodern practice because it does not seek to locate truth in one position but instead locates it on a horizon that can be approached from multiple directions. For example, when a department in the university recently pressed a scientific misconduct charge against an ESL graduate student accused of plagiarism, I was asked to serve on an arbitration committee. My knowledge of cultural differences in notions of intellectual property, the university's desire to understand and respect diversity, and the instructional needs of ESL students came together in a productive linkage to move the university toward a more complicated understanding of cultural differences in regard to the "ownership" of texts.

Articulation depends on the ability to recognize what Laclau and Mouffe call "nodal points" or issues, interests, concerns, and arguments that can be "articulated" or joined to create a more open and democratic system. Interestingly, family systems therapists also use the term *nodal points* to identify opportunities, often occurring at times of crisis or conflict, to begin moving differently in patterned relationships. As Murray Bowen (1986) explains, recognizing these nodal points comes after the hard work of differentiating a self apart from our formative relationships, of defining independent goals, and of coming to terms with the self-limiting anxiety and external pressure to "change back" that arises when one begins to move differently. The courage to move differently comes not from denying or ignoring the conflicts but from having understood their historical development and from using the intellect to recognize and name the contradictions and inconsistencies previously clouded by cultural programming.

Articulating practice does not seek to suture or close down understanding, but instead to maintain openness. Systems and relationships renew themselves by incorporating differences and maintaining openendedness. When institutions remain closed off to differences, they lose their ability to educate an increasingly diverse population of students in ways that prepare them to work in an international world. Unfortunately, the university has limited open spaces for contact and response. Its values and truths are located in traditional forms and protected from contact with the present. The centrifugal forces that institutions expect writing centers to suppress are the forces that have the potential to revitalize the system. As Bakhtin puts it, "It is necessary that heteroglossia wash over a culture's awareness of itself and its language, penetrate to its core, relativize the primary language system underlying its ideology and literature and deprive it of its naive absence of conflict" (1981, 368). Writing center workers often experience the centrifugal forces, the multivoicedness that the system seeks to contain. As gendered sites, writing centers have too often maintained silence, thereby protecting the institution from challenge and conflict rather than trusting the institution to work through acknowledged conflicts to new understandings.

In the past, writing centers have functioned more as mediators between students and the institution than as articulators of differences. When operating from a mediating position, writing centers cooperate with the overdetermined nature of discourse, its "attempt to dominate the field of discursivity, to arrest the flow of differences, to construct a centre" (Laclau and Mouffe 1985, 112). As mediators, they show students that there are *necessary* links, such as formal academic diction that is appropriate in composition class. Mediating practices attempt to suture an external and authorized version of literacy rather than to promote change. When writing centers focus on changing writers, they are generally performing a mediating function, bringing students to a greater awareness of an externally authorized literacy. Although writing center workers might learn from their students and develop a greater awareness of diverse literacies, the faculty who send the students remain unchanged. Even though students may revise their papers to conform to the singular standard, they themselves are often unchanged. A mediating approach accepts a fixed notion of literacy, a singular standard, and this closes down possibilities for an increased understanding of differences.

To distinguish between mediation and articulation, I will illustrate with the example of Hajj Flemings, an African American student who has worked with our writing center over an extended period of time. While enrolled in an advanced composition course, Hajj brought a draft of a paper to the writing center in which he had chosen to use the language of his neighborhood to evoke memories of childhood afternoons in the city. A week later, his paper was returned, marked for issues of diction, questions of appropriate word choice. Within a mediating practice, literacy is fixed, standard, and Hajj's language is not considered appropriate at the university. If writing centers support the idea that literacy is singular (even my word processor reminds me of this when it flags *literacies* as a misspelling) and if they support the work of teachers who think that students who depart from a singular standard of literacy can be "fixed" by "sending" them to the writing center, then writing centers contribute to closing the system to difference. Not only does this prevent the system from revitalizing itself, it also potentially damages individuals. When the university finds Hajj's language inappropriate, he gets the message that even though he has been admitted to the university, there is no place for him there unless he leaves his home community behind. As Hajj himself puts it,

> The purpose of signing up for this class, I thought, was to improve my writing skills not to stifle the skills that I already have. I was asked [in this assignment] to describe a place and a person. Both of my subjects came from my childhood in my old neighborhood. To accurately describe what was going on, I had to use the dialect. (Matthews and Flemings 1995)

When writing centers function as mediators and support students' efforts to revise their papers in response to teachers' suggestions, students like Hajj can find fix-it advice. But if the writing center only "helps" Hajj revise his paper to get a good grade and maintains silence about the cultural forces at work, the writing center blocks change.

Within an articulating practice, a writing center would be a place where students like Hajj find opportunities to discuss the ways that standard English is frequently linked to practices of literacy that exclude and devalue other literacies. The writing center could be a space in the university where institutionally structured racism is acknowledged, where students like Hajj can discuss the possibilities and impossibilities of negotiating cultural and racial conflicts. It is no easy matter for a white middle-class writing coach to open up a dialogue about black English. Family systems theory helps here as well. When anxiety is high, Bowen (1986) says we revert to cause/effect thinking. Our best bet in these situations is not to react emotionally or even to speculate, for example, on *why* Hajj's use of black dialect was found unacceptable. Instead Bowen says to accept *that* things like this happen and to *think* about what we want to say about them. Usually when anxiety is high, we react by blaming or by withdrawing in silence rather than applying our intellect to state our beliefs and listen to others. Within an articulating practice, the writing center task is not to confront professors or to second-guess professors' intentions but instead to think about how writing workers themselves talk with students like Hajj.

When literacy practices are examined from an articulatory view of change, their ideological and arbitrary character can be acknowledged. Writing center workers need to talk with students about academic expectations in ways that acknowledge whose values are at stake. With a student like Hajj, for example, we can acknowledge that his professor is privileging white middle-class discourse; we can ask Hajj to speculate on whether the same privileging would happen in a similar class at a historically black college; with Hajj we can search for examples of writing that mixes discourses; we can talk about the consequences of working more with Hajj's purposes than with the professor's revision instructions. Most important, we can avoid a silent professor-knows-best stance and talk about the values, ideologies, arbitrariness, and contextual constraints that bear on Hajj's decision making. Articulatory practice accepts the possibility of alternate literacies as well as the arbitrary and contingent nature of academic literacy. An articulating practice acknowledges that a dominant literacy can be perversely articulated and restricted to certain categories of the population. Articulating practice, unlike mediating practice, recognizes that because overdetermination operates on a symbolic level and has no literal reference, its linkages are partial and temporary. The linkages of articulatory practice are not *necessary* links in spite of the "constant effort to establish historical, contingent, variable links" (Mouffe 1992, 372).

A writing center that emphasizes articulatory practice seeks to maintain openness; it seeks not to protect faculty from knowledge of students but instead increases the contact. For example, writing centers are in an excellent position to invite students like Hajj to join with them in conference presentations and publications that can contribute to a professional awareness of what happens at the thresholds where literacies come into contact with one another. If writing center workers learn to think of themselves as fieldworkers curious about the liminal understandings that occur on the borders of cultural and academic practices, they can invite students to share their observations about what happens at these crossings. This move requires acknowledging that contextual institutional forces are not benign, that they seek to contain and silence differences.

Surely some readers by now are asking "What about standards?" and other readers with a more liberal bent are wondering "What will happen to students like Hajj if they don't master the dominant code?" There will always be standards. African American students know better than we do whose standards they are. The problem is that as things currently operate in writing centers, we *pretend* these standards are neutral rather than standards that favor students born into the dominant group. We do students a disservice if we withdraw from discussions about the consequences of not mastering the dominant code. But we do them an even bigger disservice if we assume that because they use a nondominant code they haven't mastered or don't know about the dominant code. We also do them a disservice if we assume we know what is best for them.

Skeptical readers may ask if writing centers, given that they are often staffed by undergraduates, are up to the transformative tasks I have outlined here. Are we simply transferring our desire for a more just society onto those most poorly situated to accomplish it? In my experience, students are both eager to and capable of assuming the roles of scholar and researcher. The naive and childlike subjectivity we have constructed for them is the chief barrier to their participation in theoretical discussions and institutional change. Some readers may believe that my experience is too locally defined, that *their* students are much

more in need of traditional remedial assistance. I invite them to read
Children of Promise (1991), an account of work that shows the transformative power of constructing differently those students we perceive
as our weakest. In this book, Shirley Brice Heath and Leslie Mangiola
share their stories of cross-age tutoring programs. One program invited
fifth graders who were nonnative speakers of English and who already
had a history of poor school performance to tutor first graders. Not only
did the first graders benefit, but the fifth graders advanced in their
conceptualization of literacy events, transferred literate behaviors from
exclusively Spanish to English, placed greater value on being literate,
developed self-confidence and leadership, and steered their tutees to
literacy activities that involved selecting books, retelling stories, sound-
ing out words, and writing their own stories. Such changes don't happen automatically; writing center directors need to be prepared to develop not only their tutors' cultural knowledge but also their critical
language and perspective.

As sites of articulating practice, writing centers will be less tuned to
helping writers master community conventions and more tuned to developing the capacity of the staff to entertain multiple perspectives, to
resist binary alignments, to think in systematic and complicated ways
about literacy practices, to manage emotional reactivity to hot issues,
to gather evidence, and to explore the contradictions in literacy work.
Defined as places of research and knowledge making, writing centers
are uniquely situated to invite undergraduates into intellectual work
that makes a difference. As sites of articulating practice, they can be institutional catalysts in the effort to rethink literacy education in ways
that no longer reproduce social divisions and that redefine what counts
as literacy in postmodern times.

Notes

1. A version of this essay originally appeared in *College Composition and
Communication* as "Rearticulating the Work of the Writing Center." I thank *CCC*
editor Joe Harris and reviewers Ed Lotto and Cynthia Lewiecki-Wilson, whose
comments helped me shape my argument. (CCC (1996) 47.4 523–48)

2. This feminization of writing center work has been analyzed by Ed Lotto,
Gary Olson, and Evelyn Ashton-Jones, and Mary Trachsel, among others.

3. Deliberately mixing popular advice about self-recovery and theoretical
analysis is the same move recently made by Gloria Steinem in the *Revolution
from Within: A Book of Self-Esteem* (1992) and bell hooks in *Sisters of the Yam: Black
Women and Self-Recovery* (1993). As activists for political and social change, both
of these women offer self-help texts with the realization that external political
change is more likely to occur when accompanied by internal personal change.

Chapter Five

Toward a Fair
Writing Center Practice

Fair adj. **1.** visually beautiful or admirable; lovely: *a fair maiden*. **2.** Of light color, as: **a.** Blond: *fair hair*, **b.** Pale or white; not ruddy; *fair skin*. **3.** Clear and sunny; free of clouds or storms: *fair skies*. **4.** Free of blemishes; unstained; clean: *one's fair name*. **5.** Regular and even: *a fair edge*. **6.** Free of obstacles; open: *fair sailing*. **7.** Promising; likely; propitious: *in a fair way to succeed*. **8.** Free of favoritism or bias; impartial: *a fair judge*. **9.** Just to all parties: equitable: *a fair compromise*.
—*The American Heritage*
Dictionary, 1979

Postmodernity is the moral person's bane and chance at the same time.
—Zygmunt Bauman,
Life in Fragments:
Essays in Postmodern Morality

I turn again to a story, this one about Keith Sawyer, one of the first students I worked with when I was hired to be a tutor in 1978. Why do I remember Keith twenty years after our work together? Although I didn't recognize this at the time, he was the first to teach me how unprepared I was and how much I had to unlearn before I could work effectively in a writing center. Keith, a white, mild-mannered, easygoing, rural Michigan college kid, and I, a serious, goal-driven former high school English teacher, worked together once a week for the academic year. I began our work together thinking that my understanding of academic writing and my desire to be helpful would be useful to Keith. Slowly, and not without a good amount of frustration, I began to see that Keith's literacy education had convinced him that he was "not a writer." He wore this constructed identity lightly, and he accepted my suggestions pleasantly, making modest efforts to implement them, yet his writing stayed safely in a mid-range—he took no intellectual or personal risks on paper.

As he shared more of himself with me, I became aware of the literacy histories that separated us, histories that began with our immigrant grandparents' choice of work, his on a farm, mine in urban "rich people's houses." In his family, talk was used for connecting; in mine, talk was often examined and critiqued for ethnic and class markers in order to assimilate, to get ahead. I was born into a language purified by two generations of assimilation efforts; he came from a family that found comfort in the familiarity of old ways. School practices were familiar to me. In school, teachers corrected my language like my parents did at home. For Keith, school had been a place where he was corrected before he was listened to, where he was told he had to learn the sanctioned code before he could contribute. School, particularly English class, had become a place where he was reluctant to open his mouth. From regular exposure to institutional practices that silenced him, Keith had learned the opposite of what literacy educators generally hope to accomplish. What we had both learned through the tacit social practices of family and school we needed to unlearn if either of us were to gain more than frustration from our work together.

From the time I was a child, I took the social structure of school for granted, and I had been rewarded for paying attention to what matters to the powerful. For me, school and home were all one struggle to assimilate, and assimilation was not only good but also necessary. I had learned, by virtue of my family's successful assimilation, to use language to mark the boundaries between Keith's group and mine. Keith, on the other hand, had learned to protect himself in school, taking care not to let its powerful practices affect him, shrugging off the labels of people who were strangers to him. While the two of us learned to laugh together and to get some work done, a year wasn't nearly long enough for me to change my assumptions about the values at work in literacy education, and until school representatives changed the negative way they constructed Keith, he was unlikely to change his interactions with literacy.

While working with Keith, I began to question the "if you really know it, you can say it" maxim when I saw how much Keith knew and how little he said because the dominant codes and practices silenced him. I found myself wanting to make a case for Keith to his teachers, to persuade them to see his brightness. As Keith resisted thinking of himself as a writer, I became aware of how conventional approaches to literacy education had taught me to make social judgments when someone used the wrong past participle. But the focus of my job was to fix Keith, to help him read and write more like the mainstream; my job wasn't to contextualize Keith's work or to argue for changes in attitudes toward students like him or to suggest changes in teaching practices. Keith—and the many equally likable students who followed him—gradually led me to the realization that the institution of higher education to which I had pledged my professional life was not fair.

Twenty years after my work with Keith, I watch a tutorial in the writing center I direct. An experienced white middle-class writing coach is working with a black working-class student. The student asks, "How should I start this assignment?" The coach responds by carefully reading and rehearsing the specifications of the assignment sheet. He points to the requirement of five sources; he asks the student if he knows why the teacher wants him to employ sensory detail (a teacherly question more than a genuine one); he calls attention to the length expected; his body language suggests he is frustrated with the student. Perhaps the writing coach is projecting his school history on the student, wondering why the student has waited so long to get started, wondering why he hasn't yet read the assignment sheet, wondering if the student expects him to do the work for him. In writing centers, "doing the work for a student" is something to avoid at all costs. Students, after all, must learn to "take responsibility for their own work."

I sense the widening gap between the student's question and the coach's frustration, and I wonder if the coach has told the student why he reads the assignment sheet so carefully or if the student understands the link between what the coach sees on the assignment sheet and his question about how he should start to write. If I followed the impulse to ask these questions I would undermine the coach's confidence in himself and in me, and I would betray the students' patient trust. To the white middle-class coach, starting with the assignment sheet is "just natural" because he is accustomed to trusting the literacy practices of the school, the good intentions of teachers, the values of higher education. Because he was born into the dominant culture, he has been rewarded for understanding and following the dominant expectations. And because his white middle-class background is congruent with the cultural milieu of school, he is able to discern what is expected in terms of topic development and structure. To him, school has been fair, and it seems intuitively obvious that one would follow directions and do what the teacher requires. To him, truth lies in the details of the assignment sheet. He has had few occasions to doubt that teachers ask students to do meaningful work. He may imagine his work in the writing center as an effort to extend and implement the good intentions of teachers.

To the student, who grew up in a different literacy and with a different view of the social structure, the value of and the reasons for this assignment may seem anything but obvious. Teachers may have rarely taken his lived experience into account. His difficulty getting started may not have anything to do with a lack of understanding or a lack of desire to do well but, as Linda Brodkey (1992) describes it, with the teacher's failure (as well as previous teachers' failures) to articulate the student's representation of himself as a subject different from his teachers. I borrow language from Brodkey here because she makes the important argument that students refuse our invitations to literacy when we literacy educators fail to take into account their differing political, social, historical, and economic histories. For Keith and for this student, whom I will call Michael, the structure of school has constructed their relationship with literacy in ways far different from mine and Michael's middle-class tutor.

Sadly, the gap between a well-intentioned writing coach and a well-intentioned student has not significantly narrowed in twenty years. Academics may be more theoretically aware of the ideological work of literacy, yet theory moves slowly toward practice. I cannot, for example, suggest to the coach that he explain to the student that literacy is ideological and that the student needs to determine the ideological function of the assignment; nor can I whip out a list of strategies for writing that derive from an ideological approach. As I watch this tutorial, I suspect that both coach and student will be frustrated at its conclusion. Still, the coach can reassure himself that he has done the right thing by "not appropriating the students' work." And even though the student might not yet see his way into the paper, he can at least assure himself that he has "taken advantage of the available resources." They can find this assurance because they both believe what we academics want to believe—that the institution is fair. Even the existence of a writing center on campus is proof that the institution is committed to improving individual performance.

Throughout this book I have been working against the common-sense theories that make it easy to position students as lacking, against the notion of academic literacy as ideologically neutral, against the tacit assumptions and practices that maintain an unfair status quo. I have also maintained that the intellectual changes of postmodernity offer unique possibilities for writing centers to rethink the contradictions of practice, contradictions that were previously hidden by modernist assumptions. In this final chapter, I turn to the distressing gap between theory and practice and argue that writing centers can work more effectively to close that gap if we accept the notion that institutional practices are not fair. Rather than continuing to hold students individually responsible for their work, writing center workers need to hold themselves responsible not only for granting students membership to the academic literacy club but also for changing the gates of that club when change is necessary.

The (In)Justice of Institutional Practices

Accepting the notion that the institution isn't always an equitable place is not easy for people like me who, from the time I was a child, wanted life to be more fair. But I'm not talking here of childlike complaints about fairness, complaints that precede the announcement that one is quitting the game. Nor am I talking about a bland sort of acceptance that overlooks or even condones injustice. I am speaking of an understanding of social justice that accounts for the notion that while most people experience some sort of domination in their everyday lives, others (way too many), by virtue of their membership in a particular group, experience not only domination but also oppression. Oppression is the form of injustice that many literacy ethnographers have documented in studies showing how tacit cultural values work against the academic success of students from nonmainstream backgrounds (see, for example, Brodkey 1989; Delpit 1995; DiPardo 1993; Fox 1994; Grimm and Penti 1998; Heath 1983; Hull et al. 1991).

Members of the dominant group have difficulty conceptualizing oppression because it lies outside their lived experience. They tend to minimize its effects because they confuse it with the injustice of domination that they regularly experience in the form of institutional hierarchical decision making. Accepting some degree of domination is usually necessary in order to get what we need from institutions: paychecks, promotions, good grades, opportunities to learn. And some domination is necessary for institutions to function effectively. Members of the dominant group are usually able to tolerate domination, accepting it as simply the way things are. Generally they accept domination indefinitely until an issue arises that makes them angry: the boss prohibits all employees from making personal calls from the workplace or the priest tells an engaged couple they can't get married in the church or the department excludes graduate students from voting on decisions that affect their working conditions.

If we are members of the dominant group, we can usually decide whether to continue under this "unfair" institutional domination. For example, we might decide to remain within the institution if we feel that the domination is temporary, or if the institutional support for our

development outweighs the constraints on our behavior, or if we believe we can express our outrage and be heard. Otherwise, we can decide to leave the particular dominating system. To members of the dominant group, institutional domination is just the way things are—one
accepts it as a condition one needs to endure in order to get what one
wants, or one leaves. Institutional domination is a fact of college student life. Students (most of them anyway) are generally enrolled in institutions of higher learning temporarily, and they understand the trade-
offs, accepting domination in return for the opportunity to learn and
earn a degree.

Institutional oppression is not the same as institutional domination. Domination is often irritating, but oppression is isolating and all-
consuming. Oppression is not temporary or escapable. Individuals experience institutional oppression simply because they are members of
a particular group. The injustice of oppression occurs in this paradoxical way: "the oppressed group's own experience and interpretation of
social life finds little expression that touches the dominant culture,
while that same culture imposes on the oppressed group its experience and interpretation of social life" (Young 1990, 60). Students from
traditionally underrepresented groups experience oppression when
they encounter *explicit* academic practices that impose the view of the
dominant culture (the exclusion of Native American/African American/
Latino experience from the curriculum) and when they encounter
implicit expectations that mark their experience as not normal (the expectation that academic writing should express rather than challenge
mainstream values). According to this distinction between domination
and oppression, it can be said that if writing centers fail to acknowledge
the culturally specific and arbitrary nature of academic expectations,
they are complicit in institutional oppression.

When I meet with groups of students from traditionally underrepresented groups on my campus, I tell them that the most dangerous assumption they can make, the one that may lead to academic failure, is
that the institution is fair. If they believe school is fair, they will judge
their work habits against the work habits of students from the dominant group, and when they run into academic difficulty, they will suffer a failure of spirit, blaming themselves for not measuring up. I tell
them directly that they will have to work harder and smarter than most
students to be successful because our university was not designed with
them in mind. Located in a geographically remote area six hundred
miles north of Detroit, Michigan Tech is a university with a predomi-
nately white, masculine, pull-yourself-up-by-your-bootstraps ethos—
individualistic, competitive, hierarchical. It is a university with a strong
respect for expertise, for quantitative data, and for empirical methods.
Some students are well suited to this environment. But if they are not

white, not male, not middle-class, not yet mathematically advanced, not competitive, not practically oriented, not able-bodied, or not heterosexual, they will have a tougher time making a place for themselves because universities do not (and probably cannot) account for all students fairly when they construct a notion of their typical student.

Iris Marion Young, a political theorist who reconsiders the concept of social justice within a postmodern context, explains that oppression is structural, "embedded in unquestioned norms, habits, and symbols, in the assumptions underlying institutional rules and the collective consequences of following those rules." Young reminds us that oppression occurs "not because a tyrannical power coerces . . . but because of the everyday practices of a well-intentioned liberal society." It is difficult if not impossible to hold individuals responsible for oppression because oppression is "a consequence of often unconscious assumptions and reactions of well-meaning people in ordinary interactions" (1990, 41). In a writing center, oppression can manifest itself in well-intentioned questions to a first-year student about whether he or she is finding the adjustment to dorm living difficult and if he or she has found any good restaurants. If the student is from a large or troubled family, the assumption that dorm living is supposed to be difficult can make a student wonder why it feels so luxurious to share a room with only one person or to feel guilty about falling asleep at night untroubled by ongoing family crises. If the student is from a poor or working-class family, he or she may feel ashamed to explain that they cannot afford a restaurant meal, particularly while living in a residence hall where meals are included. Casual questions like these, meant to establish a friendly connection, project a middle-class "normal" experience onto students, reminding them in small but significant ways that their experience is unaccounted for, that they are not normal students.

The "Difference Doesn't Matter" Argument

According to the notion of individual autonomy inscribed in autonomous literacy, one can erase differences of race, class, or ethnicity by learning a particular code. If one believes this, it is easy to excuse the fact that teachers privilege white middle-class discourse because schools promise that if one learns to think, talk, value, and write like the white middle class, then difference won't matter. This analysis, used to justify the ultimate fairness of literacy education, is faulty on at least two levels.

On one level, it implicitly condones discrimination. While we are no longer allowed to publicly discriminate against people based on race, culture, or ethnicity, it is still permissible to do so if the person's language is marked by his or her race, culture, ethnicity, and class. It obscures the realization that "linguistic bigotry is among the last publicly expressible prejudices left to members of the Western intelligentsia." According to social linguist Deborah Cameron's analysis, linguistic conventions often serve as "the last repository of unquestioned authority for educated people in secular society" (12). Although linguistic conventions are based on arbitrary rules, "the social function of the rule is not arbitrary"(Cameron 1995, 12).

To the extent that writing centers maintain policies not to edit or proofread students' papers, they are complicit in this oppressive use of literacy to rank people based on features of their language. But if literacy still works so well as a gatekeeping tool, isn't it even more important that students, regardless of their social position, learn the conventions? My answer is yes, and writing centers should hold themselves responsible not only for teaching them, but also for acknowledging their arbitrary nature and for teaching them in the context of students' writing—which for most of us will feel a great deal like editing and proofreading. Moreover, writing center directors should work toward positioning themselves where they can interrupt the institutional zealousness in this practice of social discrimination on student writing.

Some readers may think that I am arguing only about surface issues of grammar, punctuation, and spelling and, because their writing center deals more with higher-order matters of reasoning, argumentation, and evidence, that this concern doesn't apply to them. I maintain that higher-order concerns are just as arbitrary and just as embedded in one culture's ideology as the lower-order concerns. The expectation, for example, that students must develop arguments using sources indicates that only those arguments developed in other sources are worth addressing and that one's own position can always be enhanced by reference to textual authority (with the Bible being a possible exception). These are culturally specific values.

On another level, the "difference doesn't matter" argument suggests that if one learns the mainstream code, then race/class/color won't matter. Patricia Williams, author, lecturer, and professor of law at Columbia University, argues that this belief, greatly informed by liberal individualism, "constitutes ideological confusion at best, and denial at its very worst" (1997, 4). By labeling color or class as "that which makes no difference" we attempt to undo that which matters a great deal, and we (white middle-class) people do it because for us color hasn't mattered. Let me illustrate with another story how flawed this belief is. Last year, we sponsored an informal roundtable discussion about race in our writing center. During the discussion, I happened to be sitting next to an African American student who works as a coach in the writing center, a kind, intelligent, compassionate, and exceedingly well-spoken young man with a wonderful sense of humor. A member of the round-table commented that racial fear on campus was signaled in small ways, and gave as an example white students crossing to the other side of the street when they saw a black male student walking at dusk toward the residence hall. The listeners, all of them nice people who abhor prejudice, did not respond to this comment. For the rest of the talk, I was aware that the young man sitting next to me was trembling, indeed shuddering, as one who has witnessed a violent act or a horrible accident. Regardless of his character, regardless of how well-spoken and articulate he is, his color is still perceived as a threat on campus, and that, in my opinion, is an example of oppressive structural violence. Young observes, "the liberal imperative that differences should make no difference puts a sanction of silence on those things which at the level of practical consciousness people 'know' about the significance of group differences" (1990, 134).

Students from underrepresented groups experience oppression in classrooms and writing centers every day. They experience it bodily and intellectually and because the dominant group doesn't *intend* it, because underrepresented students do not feel prepared to take on the social argument against it, they remain silent. Later that year, while this same student and I visited some shops together during a break at a conference, I too felt the intensified vigilance of sales clerks when we strolled together through a store, a vigilance I never experienced while shopping with my son of the same age. Clearly for some students, difference does matter a great deal, even on a university campus where most people claim that differences make no difference. Young writes, "Group oppressions are enacted in this society not primarily in official laws and policies but in informal, often unnoticed and unreflective speech, bodily reactions to others, conventional practices of everyday interaction and evaluation, aesthetic judgments, and the jokes, images, and stereotypes pervading mass media" (1990, 148).

The Fairness of Holding Writing Centers Responsible for Just Practice

This concept of unjust structural oppression can make us uncomfortable. As individuals we cannot keep white people from crossing to the other side of the street at the sight of a black man. Nor can we even blame a friend for crossing to the other side if that action is habitual, unconscious, not intended to inflict harm. To say that oppression is structural means that individuals cannot be blamed for unconscious unjust behavior. However, individuals *can* be held responsible for changing the habits and attitudes that contribute to oppression. Young explains it this way:

> Blame is a backward-looking concept. Calling on agents to take re-
> sponsibility for their actions, habits, feelings, attitudes, images, and as-
> sociations, on the other hand, is forward-looking; it asks the person
> "from here on out" to submit such unconscious behavior to reflection,
> to work to change habits and attitudes. (1990, 151)

I believe that writing center workers need to pay much more attention to the ways institutional habits, practices, assumptions, and perspectives inadvertently oppress some students and to hold themselves
responsible "from here on out" for submitting these habits to critical
reflection.

The dominant ideology of individual liberalism that structures the
system of higher education and the writing programs and writing centers within it has historically distracted our attention from the systemic
influences on our work and instead focused our attention on the individual student who is expected to change, to become normal. As Young
explains, within an individualist ideology, we hold individuals rather
than institutions accountable. Sometimes we blame students for not
trying hard enough or not setting the right priorities or not learning
enough in high school and sometimes we blame teachers for creating
unfair obstacles or for having unfair attitudes or for not preparing students for college or sometimes we blame parents for not having the
"right" family values. I am arguing that instead we need to hold ourselves responsible for changing the cultural practices, the institutional
conditions, the unconscious habits that contribute to structural oppression. As the writing center director, for example, it is my responsibility
to reflect on the interaction I observed between Michael and his writing coach and to create the conditions for Michael's coach to reflect on
what attitudes he brings to his session, to recognize the dangers of projecting his cultural assumptions onto students who have cultural histories different from his own.

Writing centers should be a place where, as Brandt puts it, we
"grant membership" to students, "accepting them as active knowledge
users, knowledge makers, and even 'paradigm shifters'" (1990, 120).
Unfortunately, students like Keith and Michael are not granted membership but rather imagined as people who need help, people who need
the expert knowledge that tutors can provide, people who lack the
right paradigm, if they have any paradigm at all, people who need to
take individual responsibility for the impossible task of pulling themselves out of one social group and into another.

Some readers may still be thinking that it seems "only fair" to expect students from traditionally underrepresented groups to meet the

mainstream standards of the institution. And besides, isn't it simply "rhetorically effective" to learn to write with the needs and expectations of a particular audience in mind? Isn't that, after all, what all of us have to do? Isn't that the job of the writing center rather than waging war against prejudice? I am not arguing that writing centers should relax their expectations nor am I arguing that students shouldn't have to try to meet mainstream standards. Rather, I believe that writing centers can work more effectively and more fairly with students if we rethink some of our basic assumptions.

The "Demise of Power-Assisted Universals"

Fortunately, postmodernity has undermined the liberal ideology that holds students responsible for changing the social structure. We no longer have to accept the modernist emphasis on autonomous individuals who are self-made, freely choosing, existing apart from history and outside of language, a concept of the individual that obscures the injustice of oppression. But without this notion of the autonomous individual that so many writing center practices depend upon, we are confronted with the void, a void that was always there but disguised by modernity, a void that most comfortably situated people would like to continue to ignore. According to social theorist Zygmunt Bauman, *"the demise of the power-assisted universals and absolutes has made the responsibilities of the actor more profound, and indeed, more consequential, than ever before"* (italics in original) (1995, 6). As modernist foundations erode, we come face-to-face with our responsibilities as moral agents.

Giving up on the ideology of liberal individualism doesn't mean giving up on individuals, but it does require acknowledging that because institutional practices are not fair, writing center workers need to work with more awareness, more explicitness, more discomfort than before, when they were protected by the assumption that institutions were fundamentally fair. Relentless reflection on how we know what we know and why we assume what we assume creates conditions for social transformation because it weakens the confidence derived from naturalizing the ways of the dominant group. Once we enter the void created by lack of certainty, we might become, in Delpit's words, "vulnerable enough to allow our world to turn upside down in order to allow the realities of others to edge themselves into our consciousness" (1988, 297).

In postmodern times, writing center workers have more responsibility and fewer guarantees. They have to work without the expectation that a right answer can be found or that a set of principles will be located that can guide their decisions. They cannot hope that an expert will rescue them from ambivalence and responsibility. What to do? Where to turn? How to decide? Bauman reminds us that "moral selves do not discover their ethical foundations, but . . . build them up while they build up themselves" (1995, 20). If all we have available in the process of building ourselves up is the dominant normative values, then we have less hope for change, for enlarged thought, for more fair practices. But in a writing center, we have much more available. More than likely we have undergraduates doing institutional work, students who are less socialized into the dominant professional ideology and perhaps willing to rethink the status quo. More than likely we have daily encounters with Difference—with students from world majority cultures, students who have disabilities, students from traditionally underrepresented groups, students who challenge us to see our practices as bound up in one culture's perspective. But contact alone does not guarantee fair practice, particularly because of our tendency to project our experience onto others.

So how do we go about building ourselves up as moral agents; how do we work with an acceptance that some literacy practices are unfair and oppressive? How do we close the gap between the theoretical understanding of the ideological work of literacy and the daily practice of a writing center? What should we expect to find in a writing center program that is coming to terms with a loss of innocence? Readers may hope that at this point I will suggest a training curriculum for writing tutors, perhaps recommend a particular set of readings. But it's not that simple. Reading theory is not enough to dislodge faulty conceptions about literacy, nor are warmth, friendliness, and good liberal intentions enough. To function as agents of change in higher education, to work toward a fair practice, writing center workers must understand how systems function, how language influences the construction of Self and Other, how literacy works as cultural and social practice, how political action produces social change.

These understandings are not achievable in a single course but rather through an ongoing and complex interaction of theoretical critique and contact with difference along with the encouragement to reach beyond the inevitable annoyance of having one's cultural habits questioned. The aim is not to replace modernist power-assisted universals with postmodern universals but to develop the capacity of writing center workers to become theorists themselves. We used to have a handbook at our writing center that, having undergone seven revisions, was a thick collection of information about writing practices at the university, about tutoring strategies, about dos and don'ts for handling difficult situations. We realized that if we wanted the coaches to be thinkers, we had to stop doing the thinking for them. The current handbook is a collection of stories written by members of the staff about their development as theorists—stories that denaturalize expectations about what working in the writing center involves, stories about the complexities of specific coaching situations, stories about developing awareness of alternative ways to understand the world, stories about reading students and reading classroom assignments, stories about developing trust, about cultural differences, about learning disabilities, about the nature of expertise. All of these narratives, written by both graduate and undergraduate members of the staff, move back and forth between theory and practice, sometimes making direct links, sometimes indirect ones. A fair writing center practice must be constantly under revision, and the people who work in writing centers must be open to transformation, always ready to question the institution and the culture that positions them to work with people inappropriately characterized as "needing help." Without power-assisted universals, writing centers can be more effectively marketed as places where writers can seek orientation for the multidimensional task of communicating in an information-rich and culturally complex society.

From Peerness to Asymmetrical Reciprocity

For the white, middle-class, physically able people working in writing centers, learning to recognize one's assumptions as culturally bound is an important step toward more fair practice, but this is exceptionally difficult because of the many layers of normalization. Even the dictionary definition of *fair* leads us through layers of association with whiteness before it finds justice and equitable practice. When members of the dominant group mark their experience as Normal, when they unconsciously project their experience as universal, they create the conditions for unjust practice. Members of the dominant group contribute to injustice because "they fail to recognize the perspective embodied in their cultural expressions as a perspective" (Young 1990, 60). Not only do they fail to recognize it, they are exceedingly uncomfortable if it is pointed out to them.

Worse yet, members of the dominant group often believe they can suspend their experience in order to enter into the perspective of others, that through dialogue with the Other they can enter into a symmetrical, egalitarian relationship. On the contrary, as Young reminds us "each participant in a communication situation is distinguished by a particular history and social position that makes their relation asymmetrical" (1997, 39). In the haste to establish a connection of similarity or symmetry with another, we often close ourselves to the potential transformation of learning something new. Young warns, "When privileged people put themselves in the position of those who are less privileged, the assumptions derived from their privilege often allow them unknowingly to misrepresent the other's situation" (1997, 48). In writing centers we inadvertently create conditions for closure and misrepresentation when we emphasize the importance of the peer relationship in tutoring.

Young illustrates the problems that arise when one attempts or claims to take the perspective of others who are differently situated. She tells a story about how the State of Oregon initially established priorities for state funding of health care services. The initial proposal denied disabled people reimbursement for medical procedures for which able-bodied people would be reimbursed. The grounds for this decision were based on a telephone survey of Oregon citizens, designed to establish grounds for decisions about health care priorities. On the survey, many able-bodied people claimed they would rather be dead than wheelchair-bound, and this majority response was used to develop the initial regulations. Young observes that because able-bodied people project their fears of disability, they have difficulty imagining that people with disabilities find their lives worth living.

Because the funding regulations violated the Americans with Disabilities Act, they were changed; yet the story serves as a warning about the dangers of projection. If tutors are encouraged to assume a peer relationship, they risk engaging in a similar projection, representing students as similar to themselves. The assurance of peerness or symmetrical relationship can make tutors feel too secure in their judgments about students' work habits, knowledge base, motivation levels, and past experience. Confident that they can reverse perspectives, they see themselves reflected in another person, rather than perceive how the other sees them and the literacy practices of the institution. This too-ready projection closes down the potential for careful listening and attention to particular histories and perspectives.

Because we are ontologically unable to think or feel from another's perspective, a fair writing center practice should be characterized by what Young calls *wonder*, a wonder that motivates a desire to hear the Other's stories. Wonder is a humble stance of openness to the mystery of another. It starts with the assumption that there are things about another person's perspective that I cannot understand. Wonder, Young cautions us, can also be dangerous if it seeks to master the Other or turns toward voyeurism. Wonder needs to arise from a recognition that our relationships are always asymmetrical, that personal stories are inexhaustible, and that personal histories are always changing (1997, 56). In the writing center, it would mean hearing a student like Michael as genuinely not knowing how to start an assignment rather than assuming he is avoiding starting an assignment. It means we would explain how we start assignments without automatically assuming we are doing it the right way or correct way or the way that Michael would find useful.

Because writing centers are often staffed by undergraduates, much attention has been focused on the potential of the *peerness* of their relationships to the detriment of both the undergraduates who use writing centers and those who work in writing centers. Whether or not a writing tutor feels she is in a position of institutional power, the students who walk into a room institutionally labeled "Writing Center" automatically construct the tutors sitting inside the room as having institutional authority. Establishing a peer relationship within that construction is difficult, if not dishonest and impossible. Peer tutors often get caught between the pressure to assume a relationship of solidarity with students and the students' expectation that they have some sort of expertise. Entangled in conflicting roles, tutors can further mystify school success because they are unsure of how to represent the authority of academic culture. Writing center researcher Ann Kitalong-Will (1998) discovered that a tutor's choice of pronouns can reveal confusion about how to represent academic expectations. A suggestion for revision can be represented as something "*you* will want to do" or something "*we* generally do" or something "*they* do" within one half-hour tutorial. Without encouragement to think through the conflict created by the expectation of peerness versus the expectation of institutional expertise, the tutor misses opportunities to articulate whose cultural values are being advanced and why.

A fair writing center practice would acknowledge the ways writing center work positions undergraduates (and the entire staff) within the culture of power. It would find ways to explicitly acknowledge that privilege as well as to call attention to ways our cultural position might blind us to other possibilities and perspectives. When I work in the writing center with a fellow faculty member who is African American, I need to remember our lack of peerness as well as the ways people of my race stand in a relation of historical oppression to people of her race. Given the differences in our personal and cultural histories—including that she holds a higher professional rank than I do and that her expertise is in a field quite different from mine—her willingness to ask me to work with her is at once an act of courage and practicality and vulnerability.

Undergraduate writing tutors regularly face similar situations in their daily encounters. Remembering their personal, cultural, and historical limits, learning to deliberately call attention to what they don't know and to their own habits of performance is crucial to navigating the contact zone. If all this is submerged and silenced under the concept of peerness and innocence in writing center training, it will emerge in body language and in silent judgments. It would be more fair, for example, for Michael's writing coach to take into account that he and the student do not share the same cultural assumptions, the same history, or the same relationship to school. As a student who is comfortable in school and who knows how to negotiate its demands, the tutor must learn to articulate the often hidden cues that tell him how to maneuver within the constraints of an assignment. This does not demand a mastery of a new language but a heightened self-awareness. It requires the honesty to recognize one's difference, particularly one's entitlements and one's cultural and institutional power. Michael's writing coach probably didn't consider the option just described because he listened to Michael's request in the way we are culturally disposed to listen: we project our experience on others; we listen with predetermined categories.

Learning to see one's perspective *as* perspective is more likely to happen if writing centers are staffed by people from diverse majors and diverse backgrounds. The common practice of hiring English and education majors is not likely to produce this mix. Nor is the practice of screening applicants for their high GPAs. Learning to take risks in recruitment is essential to forming a writing center staff that not only looks like a place that students from different backgrounds can trust but also accustoms students from mainstream backgrounds to working with people whose cultural, class, and racial histories are different from their own. This means we cannot automatically screen out applicants whose language is marked by these different histories. If I had not hired Rebecca (the rural working-class student I wrote about in Chapter 2) as a writing coach, we would never have benefited from her talent and fresh approach. Because of her own struggles with writing classes, she had developed the ability to "read" a context and determine the hidden expectations. She was willing to ask real questions, ones that often seemed too direct to middle-class coaches. Her intense curiosity about people and her joy in meaningful work made her a popular writing coach. Not without a good deal of worry, I took another risk when I hired Shuhua Wang, a young woman from China. Shuhua had to negotiate difference with every student who sat down next to her. "Hello," she'd say, "My name is Shuhua, and you must be wondering how a Chinese person can help you with your writing." Wang's experience living in vastly different cultures and her nonnative's awareness of English language and culture were put to good use with each student she worked with, thus overcoming the reluctance of many mainstream students to work with someone whose English is accented.

To move toward a more "fair" writing center practice, writing centers may also have to rethink the ethical codes and policies that place limits on what tutors are allowed to do for students. Ethical codes in writing centers, particularly those that support minimalist "hands-off" tutoring, often protect those who are favorably positioned within the institution from coming to terms with the realization that the institution itself is not fair. Within a modernist context, we legislate ethics, believing that those with more education, particularly those who had been thoroughly socialized in a dominant culture or profession, could somehow legislate the behavior of others. But attempts to control the behavior of others, to submit others to a universalizing gaze, rarely achieve what they intend. While ethical codes justify the behavior of some, providing them with institutional guarantees of correct practice, they rarely serve those not favorably positioned in the institution nor do they succeed in controlling the behavior of members who choose to operate outside the guarantee.

Cultural Habits That Deny Membership

The adjective *comfortable* is frequently associated with America's vast middle class. Calling oneself middle class is a way of announcing that one is aligned with mainstream cultural values, that one is relatively financially secure, that one's health insurance assures that if one becomes *un*comfortable physically or psychologically, one can seek expert assistance. Yet underlying that comfortable middle position is an uneasiness, a fear that comfort can be lost, stolen, or undermined. Many cultural habits protect that comfort, avoiding situations that produce discomfort, turning to indirect communication when situations make us uncomfortable, and inadvertently sidelining the people who make us uncomfortable.

One of my favorite *Farside* cartoons depicts a laboratory with dogs standing around in lab coats studying locks, gate latches, and doorknobs. I think writing centers can capture the spirit of this cartoon by working with students to acknowledge what matters to the culture of power, to locate these matters in cultural preferences, and to investigate and play with possibilities of redesigning the gates. We can put to the test the mechanisms by which some of us are kept outside and imagine alternatives. To do this, we need to develop a willingness to study that which makes us uncomfortable.

Because having our cultural assumptions challenged creates discomfort, I think writing center workers need to take special notice of the students who make them uncomfortable. Often the opportunities to work toward more fair practice occur in tutorial moments of uneasiness or embarrassment, states that signal a rupture in the work of autonomous literacy. Marsha Penti, for example, discovered the motivation for her dissertation research in a writing center encounter with a student who had a strong religious identification. Penti moved from her initial discomfort in working with a student whose literacy was so different from the mainstream into a dissertation that studied the encounters between local Apostolic Lutheran students and the composition efforts of Michigan Tech's humanities department. This religious group, which has a strong presence in the local area, believes in traditional gender roles and shuns television and movies. In spite of their strong local presence, Apostolic students had been generally unaccounted for by teachers using texts that presume media literacy. In her research Penti discovered that composition scholars in general either ignore religious identification or provide primarily negative representations of religiosity. Yet in her collaboration with Apostolic students, she found that many of them excel as students because of their strong work ethic and because they generally have much more extensive reading experience than students raised in homes with televisions. Her dissertation had immediate social impact on campus, creating more awareness of the conflicts created by our naturalized assumptions about the knowledge students bring to school and about religious identity. Her interactions with this group of students also complicated their previous negative assessment of the humanities department.

Another cultural attitude that interferes with fair practice is our belief in the progressive nature of human development. As the autonomous individual moves through childhood and adolescence into adulthood, he is expected to become more serious, more comfortable with himself, and, sadly, less playful. Once we have reached adulthood, we imagine ourselves as having an intact, fully formed identity, a belief that unfortunately closes off possibilities for creative living. Nancy Welch's (1997) work is useful for her ability to read the story of the autonomous individual posited in American ego psychology against the story told by object relations theorists, who extend the concept of development throughout adulthood. Object relations theorists emphasize that forms of childhood play should never be abandoned. Using stories from a writing center, Welch incorporates object relations theory into tutoring, stressing the possibilities for creative play with individual beliefs and cultural forms. Drawing especially on the work of D. W. Winnicott, Welch refuses to approach writers from a sense of deficit but instead finds ways to make the assignment itself an object of play. Assignments are not a reality principle demanding compliance but an invitation to questioning and experimentation. Gaps between an assignment and a student are not ones to eliminate but rather to investigate and appreciate.

To work more effectively and more fairly with differences that matter, we also need to develop communication practices that do not initially feel "right" or "comfortable." Telling students directly how the culture of power works means telling them what an academic reader expects in an analysis. As Helen Fox (1994) explains to world majority students, it means they need to sound both assertive and reasonable, both confident and polite. It means they need to think about the value systems of a Western academic reader. It means we need to demonstrate how to take a topic apart in detailed rather than general ways. It means explaining what kind of evidence is considered reputable. It means we need to motivate students to write enough drafts so that by the final one their arguments are as transparent to an academic reader as possible. Most important, we need to acknowledge that these expectations are quite arbitrary. Even though they may seem to be the "right" way to do things in the academic context, in another context they are quite strange.

According to Lisa Delpit, being told the codes of power makes it easier to acquire that power, but those of us with the most power are often least aware of the codes—we believe there are simply "natural" ways of doing things (1995, 24). We feel threatened when someone questions the codes. Delpit also observes that those with "liberal" beliefs tend to believe that making the rules explicit interferes with individual agency and freedom, so they resort to indirect communication to deemphasize their power (26–27). She illustrates with reference to the indirect communication practiced by middle-class parents. She explains that these parents are likely to direct a child to get ready for bed by asking "Isn't it time for your bath?" In contrast, Delpit shares the story of her friend who tells her eight-year-old son, "Boy, get your rusty behind in that bathtub." Delpit observes that if her friend had asked a question instead, the child would have interpreted it as a true alternative rather than a parental imperative (34). Delpit explains, "the attempt of a teacher to reduce an exhibition of power by expressing herself in indirect terms may remove the very explicitness that the child needs to understand the rules of the new classroom culture" (34–35). The veiled commands of teachers and indirect suggestions of tutors often confuse students, contributing to unfair practices. Frequently, writing center tutors were raised in the dominant practices and are unaccustomed to explaining how those practices work. When students don't respond to indirectness, they are labeled "resistant to suggestion."

Cultural habit is strong enough that contact with difference alone will not suffice to change people's view of the social order or undermine a person's confidence in liberal individualism. Writing center practice needs the relentless self-reflection that questions the confidence we have in the rules of the academic literacy club. How do we know what we know? Why do we make particular assumptions about students? When we make a suggestion for revision, can we explain why? If we suggest that a student look at more sources before continuing working on his paper, can we explain why academics value the ability to write from sources? Can we end all of our suggestions for revision with a "because" statement? If we want to make the rules of power explicit and tutor in socially just ways, then we need to understand the assignments that students bring to writing centers as cultural artifacts. These assignments don't just arrive out of the blue. They have a social history; they carry implicit institutional and cultural values. In order to counteract the hidden uses of power, writing center workers need to be much more explicit about what values the assignments are trying to teach, about what teachers generally do, about how school works. And this is no comfortable task because it forces us to acknowledge the arbitrariness of academic practices and the possibility that these practices unintentionally oppress some students.

From Service to Collective Action

Postmodernism often strikes fear into the hearts of people who have been favored within institutions. They may feel that without universal principles or absolute truths or the autonomous self, anything goes, and doing the right thing no longer matters. Faced with choices in the context of eroding foundations, we become even more susceptible than ever to the demands of the marketplace. If we can no longer be certain that tutoring for academic success is necessarily the "right" thing to do or that an ethic of care is an adequate basis for a tutoring program or that the best way to define our work is "individualized instruction," then how do we decide what to do about the never-ending demand for increased services and expanded programs? The new dean wants a peer mentoring program that might compete with the existing writing center. An African American student organization wants to develop a separate learning center. The department wants a course in service learning that sends tutors into community service organizations. These pressing demands are made more complicated by a context in which resource allocation is more closely tied to accreditation and assessment results. Would it be worthwhile to have my writing center professionally accredited? Does it matter if the writing center director has faculty status? Is it important to have a course to train my tutors? Should I adopt one of the training texts on the market, create a handbook of my own, make do with a combination of both? Does it matter if my tutors are full-time professionals, graduate students, undergraduates, or volunteers? Should my writing center provide for electronic delivery of services?

In the upheaval created by postmodern conditions, a busy writing center director turns to the self-styled theorist to ask, "So what do I do tomorrow? What should my tutors read? How do I make these decisions?" If the most sensible advice is to pay attention to local conditions, *does it even matter* what we decide? Why not just respond to whoever has the loudest voices, the biggest budget? the newest approach? the most convincing argument?

In the absence of guarantees, the modernist is more likely to be anxious than hopeful. Paradoxically, the ability to imagine a hopeful future was limited by the modernist perspective. Patricia Williams writes,

> I do think that to a very great extent we dream our worlds into being. For better or worse, our customs and laws, our culture and society are sustained by the myths we embrace, the stories we recirculate to explain what we behold. I believe that racism's hardy persistence and immense adaptability are sustained by a habit of human imagination, deflective rhetoric, and hidden license. I believe no less that an optimistic course might be charted, if only we could imagine it. (1997, 16)

If only we could imagine it. . . .

With the erosion of guarantees in the knowable self, in individual autonomy, in the rightness of reason, and in the logic of universality comes the opportunity to begin imagining a hopeful future. Postmodernity presents writing center workers with the opportunity to connect their work with a vision of democracy that takes Difference into account. The writing center is the place to ask how the institutional practices of literacy can be made more democratic. Because writing centers are places where literacies come in contact with one another, they offer powerful educational opportunities for the social transformation that can occur when different ideologies interact. Granting membership to students means putting aside the missionary narrative of literacy, the modernist belief that we can all come together through a purified standard language. Rather, we come together when we alter our perspectives in order to perceive another's world. Granting membership means we move beyond the common mode of service to autonomous literacy to a model of public service that "focuses not on 'helping' others but on joining them as relative equals in a common project of social change" (Schutz and Gere 1998, 146). An example of such public action for me occurred recently at a writing center conference where Sylvia Matthews, a writing center administrator, and Hajj Flemings, a writing center student, presented a jointly written paper about Hajj's efforts to include Black Vernacular English in a personal essay he was writing in an advanced composition class, efforts that his teacher had not understood. Hajj decided to end their presentation with an oral performance of Langston Hughes' poem, *Theme for English B*. He stepped out from behind the podium, moved closer to the audience, and

confidently recited the poem, making an indelible mark on the conference history of white middle-class academics. Surely writing center
professionals can create more opportunities for such literacy events.

There is no set of texts, no curriculum that will prepare writing
center tutors to challenge what they have always taken for granted.
Reading theory can give them the ability to analyze too-familiar structures and to imagine alternative practices, and some theorists, like Iris
Young and Jane Flax, provide the hopeful vision that postmodern times
desperately need. Writing center work will offer them participant roles,
the opportunity to construct themselves differently. The greatest motivation will come from working side by side with students like Joe, Patty,
Mary, Hajj, Rebecca, Keith, Nancy, Michael—students whose stories remind us that the system is not fair, that racism and classism are institutionalized, and that much remains to be done in literacy education if we
take responsibility for making democracy work. In order to suggest
work of social change that writing centers might undertake, I invited
my friend and colleague Nancy Barron to end this book with some of
the stories she has told me in writing center conversations, stories that
challenge the usual hegemonic story of education as assimilation.

The students I have worked with in the writing center have motivated this book. I owe them more than a simple thank-you. For them,
I end this book with a call for change. Students tell stories every day in
writing centers. Taken together, these stories can provide all of us in
higher education with an understanding of the ways we might make
literacy education more socially responsible and more open to the needs
and desires of the real people who pay and work for an education. I
hope that this book has not been read as a new grand narrative of writing center theory or as something to be "applied" in writing centers.
Rather, I hope that it is read as an invitation to reconsider the work of
writing centers in higher education, to imagine a practice where social
justice replaces pale versions of fairness.

Afterword

As an underrepresented student, I get the feeling that those who haven't experienced school from outside the mainstream may think we don't work hard enough, don't care very much, give up too easily, and are quick to blame everyone and everything around us. Most involuntary minorities I know, and I include myself, sometimes are just tired of battling what seems to be the same blindness, the same elitism, the same ignorance, the same ethnocentric values that exclude who we are as beings in the name of learning. But before proceeding, I need to define *involuntary minority*, a term I'm borrowing from anthropologist John Ogbu.

For Ogbu, voluntary minorities are immigrants who came and continue to come to this country with the intent to assimilate and become part of the mainstream. The recent influx of Asian and eastern European students fall into this category, as do the European immigrants who passed through Ellis Island. Involuntary minorities are those who were born in this country but are not included among the majority nor among mainstream structures. The three groups Ogbu defines as involuntary minorities are the Native Americans, African Americans, and Latinos from the Southwest and West. The group I identify with are Latinos, more specifically those of Mexican descent in the West and Southwest. This group is affected by the older Chicano fabric that offers a familiar pattern and a weight heavy from bicultural political and social experience offering some security for newer Latino immigrants. Chicano culture, embedded throughout California, began after the treaty with Mexico in 1848 (Guadalupe y Hidalgo). For lots of Chicano and newer Mexican immigrant students, this means we live with a cultural template layered with 150 years of Mexican and Anglo fights and fusions that affect everything from the family to the menu, from teaching to learning.

Sometimes I know I'd be better off as a student if I'd sever my tongue, repress my experiences, and pretend to agree that everything an instructor asks is good for me. In the writing center I should turn a deaf ear to students' direct and indirect descriptions of the pressures of being the only involuntary minority in class. I should dismiss the tension I feel while a student shows me work that is a deliberate attempt to match the perceived expectations of the instructor. The words are stilted, the voice mechanical, but according to the instructor's comments on the last draft, the student's work is now following the assignment. But I can't pretend, proceed, or go along with an assignment when I see embarrassed students looking down at the table, when I feel the shame of failure, when I hear soft tight voices with a resonance of defeat.

When professors and writing coaches with good intentions stumble in front of involuntary minority students, they expect the students to show patience and explain why the well-intended actions don't work. I often hear, "How am I supposed to know if I'm being offensive when the student doesn't let me know?" And dang, if them involuntary minority students don't resist and become difficult to reach, don't they? When a mainstream academic finds herself in front of disappointed frowns, detached or unresponsive looks, or any "resistant" behavior, she most likely became, from the students' perspective, number seventy-seven times seven in a long line of academics whose good intentions failed. Working with Different frameworks isn't easy, but since involuntary minorities keep showing up in classrooms there's still time and reason to continue trying. Most involuntary minorities are used to the odd assumptions made by instructors, but it doesn't mean we've got a handle on feeling objectified or we'd graduate in higher numbers. So let's just forget it, and be on our way? No, let's just remember it and work toward new possibilities for listening and learning from instructor and student positions. Just as students protect themselves by shutting down or quitting, teachers who give up on Difference only perpetuate the constructed situations we're currently mishandling. The big difference, however, is that instructors are the ones empowered, while the students' power is to resist, maybe to fight (but this is a sure sign of academic suicide), or to walk away in frustration after failing to communicate.

School is a choice, an option, an opportunity I'll fight for if the road becomes blocked. But I don't see education tied with intelligence, as a marker of a better person. From my experience, some Latino students view school as a means to learn *separately* from grades and degrees. And more important, the instructor's and writing coach's character—their person, their patience as a teacher—first determines whether I can trust them before learning can happen. With trust I can ask an embarrassing question. I'm willing to talk to a writing coach or the instructor when I've failed to understand rather than connecting the dots and hoping my picture matches the directions on the assignment sheet. But, if I can't talk to the person in front of me, and I'm being pushed to write something opposite of what I'm trying to explain, then I shut down. I'm not even good at agreeing for the sake of agreement. I sit and scramble through my bag of examples, searching for an analogy, another window into my meaning, but only if I trust the person, and if they show a willingness to listen and a willingness to admit they don't understand because *they* can't.

Most Latinos I know are good at leaving a situation as a sign of disagreement. We make a fuss by walking away. As an undergraduate, it made me extremely uncomfortable to spend time on a task put together by an individual I no longer respected. I felt like a peon down on my knees saying "yessir" because he wore the title of teacher. Although I didn't do well in those courses, I continued in school because I believed that there was a lot yet to learn. My work now as a writing coach is a constant reminder of my own struggles with schooling in general.

I work with a variety of coaches and students and every now and then I meet an involuntary minority who expresses my own undergraduate views of school. Recently I heard from two African American students in separate courses that their instructors were "nice" but not anyone they'd feel comfortable talking to. In both cases, I think a traditional coaching strategy would be to dismiss the students' complaints and tell them to get their work done no matter what. But I couldn't because their expressed attitudes, their quick class descriptions, and their body language when they talked about their instructors told me that they didn't want to work for a person they weren't sure of. They didn't trust their instructors. And this I understand well.

I also know, however, that in the long run, the students' pride, dignity, and self-esteem need to be recognized and addressed by academics as well as how to meet the requirements of the course. Or they fail. I understand this well, too. So I asked the best resources I know and found myself quizzing two undergraduate coaches, one Anglo mainstream, the other African American. I talked to the coaches separately on different days and I knew from previous discussions that both students have relatively high GPAs, and both have complained about "difficult teachers." I asked as directly as possible, "How do you get through a course when you dislike the instructor's approach, the instructor's assignments, and the instructor's lectures?" The mainstream coach quickly and sincerely responded, "I never let my feelings for an instructor affect my grade for the course." She was frank and confident. I sat blank. I couldn't imagine such a separation. When I asked the African American coach, he responded, "That's tough. But you have to keep reminding yourself that this teacher doesn't mean anything to you. That your grade is going to get you on to better things." He sounded like the other successful coach, except he admitted that writing courses were the most difficult to get through because in math and science courses, "the answer key is in the back of the book. And in the end, you know you're right no matter what the teacher says." Writing, of course, doesn't have an answer key.

For me and other Latino students I know, the mainstream reward structure is good, but not a priority. Most of us don't go to school to get

straight A's. That's nice and great when it happens, a reason to celebrate, but grades aren't exactly associated with learning. The line
"What did you learn today?" is a question I still hear from family and
friends. "What are you learning over there?" isn't "How are your
grades?" No one is interested in my grades as long as I'm passing. My
identity isn't tied up in the grade. I know I've learned more from challenging classes that I probably pulled a B or B/C in. And I dropped the
"easy" courses because I wanted to learn, not to get an A. I was torn between regret and satisfaction when the time came for me to apply to
graduate school. I made sure every letter of intent contained the line
"My grades do not reflect my ability to perform" because my GPA was
never very high. My regret is that I couldn't imagine how important the
letter grade would be.

Grades open and close doors, but I couldn't see myself needing the
grade so badly that my dignity would have to wait. There I was, however, sitting opposite a Latino administrator of a potential department
in which I wanted to conduct my graduate studies. The department was
part of a nationally renowned prestigious university, and there I sat,
with all the heart and sincerity I was willing to part with, holding on
to the transcripts that revealed my 2.75 undergraduate academic history. I didn't have extra funds for all the application fees, so I scouted in
person, reading up on the programs' offerings and talking to officials.
When this administrator looked over my transcripts he zeroed in on my
accumulative GPA. He said, "No." Now that I think about that smoggy
day, I still carry some frustration because I didn't have the words to
express my undergraduate experience, an experience that included
entire days when no one spoke to me and I sometimes spoke to myself because the students looked away. I'm not ashamed of my school
experience because my family's dignity isn't tied to school performance. If anything, I was embarrassed and not sure why I was constantly excluded from group work. I didn't know how to talk about the
instructors who told jokes about Mexicans, about the race outbreaks
on campus, about the university paper used as a vehicle for a mainstream middle-class ultra-conservative Republican-influenced Anglo
voice that made it clear we weren't welcome. A mainstream student
openly told me that my attending school meant I kept a qualified student out. Even though I worked up to three part-time jobs to pay for
school, I was an involuntary minority. To mainstream Others, this
meant I was there on a free ride, most likely on "colored money"
(meaning grants and scholarships set aside for students of color) and
basically a token, a quota for a history many of the Anglo mainstream
insisted they had nothing to do with because they weren't alive then.
All this I wish I could have said to the administrator with the slight
smile, few words, and a definite "No." He said no to my inquiry about

graduate school. He discouraged me from applying because of a simple number, my 2.75.

I don't believe in excuses, in blaming others for my own difficulties with school and with academics. But there certainly are "extras" included in being Other. The two extremes I encountered were either I'm a hindrance taking up a privileged spot of a more worthy student; or I'm a thing, a poster child for Difference who needs saving. I'm neither. I have yet to meet anyone who fits any neatly defined category.

Am I calling for more instructors of color? Sure, that would be great, but color isn't going to solve these issues I raise. It's understanding the situations of Difference coming together. We're stuck on color because color still is a deciding factor in what the American experience will be. Economics, education, and time in this country do not grant the same privileges for people of color. African Americans, for instance, should be fully assimilated because they're not immigrants, or new to the country. African Americas should be part of the mainstream because of the established laws for their full participation during the nineteenth century and, more recently, during the mid-twentieth century. But, color is still part of the problem. In writing center work, even if the coach and student are from the same background, even if the coach understands and identifies, the student may still not be able to overcome the challenges of school. Here's a complicated story I recently experienced and continue to reflect upon.

I worked with Sam (not his real name) in the writing center for almost two years. Sam was a Latino student from southern California. We met during his first year, my third at Michigan Tech. I met Sam under circumstances I wouldn't have met any other new Tech student. His well-intentioned instructor sought me out and had the student follow him until he found me. We were introduced to each other because we were both Latino, both from southern California. It was an awkward moment. Me, a Latina, twelve years his senior; him, a Latino, a first-term eighteen-year-old. True to the cultural rules I'm familiar with, he behaved like a younger person in my presence. He was typically polite, looked down, spoke only when spoken to, and, besides that, he was shy. The instructor actually prodded us to talk while he stood by and watched. I told the student in Spanish that his instructor was fastidioso y un irritante. It would take a term before Sam decided to come to the writing center to work with me, and I wasn't surprised. I wouldn't want to go work with someone the instructor dragged me over to see. The instructor didn't know the student, and he didn't know me. But he meant only good, so I'm supposed to thank him or feel sorry for the instructor. I went numb toward him instead. I had nothing to say.

I learned what dorm life was like for Sam. Initially he laughed at the stereotypes his Anglo friends imposed on him: Gang member, drive-by shooter, anything negative from the Latino community and East Los Angeles. The student and I worked on his writing and he continued to come until the spring term of his second year. He was well prepared for college courses but not for college life. Sam knew to take notes, to study and review, to write and rewrite. His papers got written, and he got feedback from me or the walk-in writing coach. He came to Tech with strategies for academic success, but not for academic life. He walked a blurry line of school work and school climate, and eventually our fragile network shattered. He left Tech.

We seemed the perfect match: two Latino students from the West, specifically from southern California, one the writing coach, the other a student in need. But he left. He struggled, he worked hard, and dealt with a lot of small but meaningful incidents from peers and family. His writing coach was one person among many others. I got as busy as he did, and we naturally had different interests. He faced struggles I never did and probably won't. He never told me how close he was to leaving; I never read a hint of his packing up to go. There are many "Maybe I should've" points in my reflecting on this experience, but I think more of what actually was in place. What I *did* do and say, what else was being said and done. His story is his own to tell in detail. I can only tell my portion, and as a coach I'm reminded of the "Fannie and Morgan" story Anne DiPardo shared. I use and refer to that chapter many times, and now I wonder what else was happening to Fannie. The student I worked with wrote decently, he always wrote on topics of personal interest, and his motivation swayed according to his school experiences.

Defining Difference is one thing; recognizing Difference is another; feeling Different is difficult to write about. It isn't easy because being an underrepresented student means I'm different in all my courses, in everything that I do and am at the university. Since writing is deeply tied to public and private identity, it poses a particularly difficult challenge to me and to students like me who are trying to figure out who we are to our teachers, who they are as teachers, and how we can succeed. And of all the help at the university, it is the writing center that is best positioned to help students and teachers reevaluate assumptions, create understanding, and prepare for the possibilities that nonmainstream students present.

When Nancy asked if I would contribute an afterword for her book that would move the conversation about writing center work deeper into issues of diversity and difference, I wasn't sure what she was asking for. Did she want me to write about the obvious lack of historical knowledge most instructors and writing coaches have about involuntary minorities? Did she want me to write about the lack of self-reflection on the part of the mainstream? Or the refusal to accept that the mainstream are a group of people who benefit from an institutional culture deeply rooted in race and gender? Or maybe how I see school, and how I'm used to hearing other involuntary minorities talk about academics? I know a real discussion on Difference takes more than a section like an Afterword. I was told "a little cultural knowledge is a dangerous thing" and I sometimes think I see the consequences when I hear and read about Difference, and I usually only see the same few people cited (Anzaldua, hooks, Kingston, Rodriguez, Villanueva). No instructor would allow me to use the same authors, the same books, for my research on composition—although I think it would be fun to stick with the same crowd of "killer B's" (Bleich, Berlin, Brodkey, Bizzell, Bartholomae). I could say they're insightful and respected and citing them is good enough to show I know about composition.

It's important to understand that I'm writing about consequences, about real experiences that are usually forgotten or repressed when school becomes overwhelming. Most Latino students I've worked with enter the classroom neutral. Like other students, they walk in expecting the assignments, deadlines, and explanations. But the Latino community doesn't have a whole lot of role models using a bachelor's degree to "get ahead." In general, we're largely working class, moving ahead not by school but by doing our jobs well. We do, however, have a very long history of experiences with academic insensitivity, poorly supplied classrooms, and a view of learning dependent on the grade. And most of what I've shared with you here is tacit knowledge. We know because that's how schools are, that's how teachers are, that's how Anglos are, that's how writing centers are. We may not know the instructor, but we know the position. We know what the position has the power to do, and we feel it more strongly than we can articulate. We aren't very good at accusatory remarks, so mostly we stay silent. Is it really so surprising when a student responds, "I don't know" to most inquiries? Personally, *I don't know* why instructors write certain assignments. Their purpose isn't clearly written out. The students are expected to write, and write well, then hand it in. Sometimes I hear coaches ask, "How do you think you did on your paper?" and I hear the "I don't know." Makes sense to me. Students who've experienced failure in writing classes know their writing is dependent on the instructor's perspective. I know I've written a good paper when I'm familiar with what the instructor wants. Even though we're not supposed to write for the instructor, we all know there *are* parameters we write in. Just as avoiding eye contact is sometimes considered to Anglos as a sign of boredom or not paying attention rather than respect, the "I don't know" isn't necessarily a sign of being uninterested; it could well be a hint that the student isn't confident his writing matches the assignment.

If writing centers want to work with diverse students, they need to remember that diversity is more than a topic, more than a subject, more than a book, more than having friends who are Different. The good intentions from instructors and writing coaches are nice, but all they do is take the initial sting out of the eventual pain. This doesn't mean, however, that attempts or good intentions should remain silenced or dismantled because an academic lacks experience. Sensitivity doesn't mean a person needs to be multilingual or multicultural. Learning to listen differently doesn't mean the academic needs to be a world traveler, or live in a diverse neighborhood. A willingness to work with someone who may not be able to articulate her experiences means old-fashioned patience is required. The risky part is to continually reflect, and examine why a rule is rule. What assures the academic that she is right? When does the writing coach say, "That's just how it's done." Who said? Who decided? What's the price? I'm asking for everything, right? Well, not really, not yet. I haven't figured what "everything" is yet. But I do know that there needs to be a kind of patience that means more than listening because all words carry historical, social, and cultural meanings. A diverse student population means a diverse use of historical, social, and cultural frameworks. We don't all see school the same way. We don't see success and failure the same way. We don't seem to "get it" because we *don't*. We *aren't* mainstream students. The underrepresented students I identify with do see school as a place to learn and prepare for positions outside the university. Writing centers are the best place for one-to-one attention, a place where writing center coaches can share school strategies. In turn, writing centers also need to be a place where nonmainstream students can explain the understandings of time, family, and culture that create the need for different strategies.

We need academics to bring their tacit rules and expectations into explicit discussions, to give us a chance to hear and reflect on the thinking that produced the expectations. And for every successful student interaction, for every time an underrepresented student's words or actions contribute to a better understanding, those insights need to move outside of the writing center. The knowledge gained from one-to-one work ought to be in the front, in the face of administrators who may be deciding on funding, deciding on curriculum, deciding on graduate school admissions. This readily available knowledge has the potential to change the system that emphasizes our differences in unproductive ways.

Nancy G. Barron, Michigan Technological University

Works Cited

Althusser, Louis. 1971. *Lenin and Philosophy and Other Essays.* New York: Monthly Press.

Anzaldua, Gloria. 1987. *Borderlands.* San Francisco: Spinsters.

Atwood, Margaret. 1993. *The Robber Bride.* New York: Doubleday.

Bakhtin, M. M. 1981. *The Dialogic Imagination,* edited by Michael Holquist, translated by Caryl Emerson and Michael Holquist. Austin, TX: University of Texas Press.

Barthes, Roland. 1972. *Mythologies.* New York: Hill and Wang.

Bartholomae, David. 1993. "The Tidy House: Basic Writing in the American Curriculum." *Journal of Basic Writing* 12 (1): 4–21.

Barton, Ellen L. 1997. "Literacy in (Inter)Action." *College English* 59: 408–37.

Bauman, Zygmunt. 1995. *Life in Fragments: Essays in Postmodern Morality.* Oxford: Blackwell.

Bizzell, Patricia. 1988. "Arguing About Literacy." *College English* 50 (2): 141–53.

———. 1991. "Marxist Ideas in Composition Studies." In *Contending with Words: Composition and Rhetoric in a Postmodern Age,* edited by Patricia Harkin and John Schilb, 52–68. New York: Modern Language Association.

Bloom, Lynn Z. 1996. "Freshman Composition as a Middle-Class Enterprise." *College English* 58 (6): 654–75.

Bowen, Murray. 1986. *Family Therapy in Clinical Practice.* Northvale, NJ: Jason Aronson.

Brandt, Deborah. 1990. *Literacy as Involvement: The Acts of Writers, Readers, and Texts.* Carbondale, IL: Southern Illinois University Press.

———. 1995. "Accumulating Literacy: Writing and Learning to Write in the Twentieth Century." *College English* 57: 649–68.

Brodkey, Linda. 1989. "On the Subjects of Class and Gender in 'The Literacy Letters.'" *College English* 51 (2): 125–41.

———. 1992. "Articulating Poststructural Theory in Research on Literacy." In *Multidisciplinary Perspectives on Literacy Research,* edited by Richard Beach, Judith L. Green, Michael L. Kamil, and Timothy Shanahan, 293–318. Urbana, IL: National Council of Teachers of English.

———. 1995. "Writing Permitted in Designated Areas Only." In *Higher Education Under Fire: Politics, Economics, and the Crisis of the Humanities,* edited by Michael Berube and Cary Nelson, 214–58. New York: Routledge.

Bruffee, Kenneth A. 1984. "Peer Tutoring and the 'Conversation of Mankind.'" In *Writing Centers: Theory and Administration*, edited by Gary A. Olson, 3–15. Urbana, IL: National Council of Teachers of English.

Butler, Judith. 1990. *Gender Trouble: Feminism and the Subversion of Identity*. New York: Routledge.

———. 1997. *The Psychic Life of Power: Theories in Subjection*. Stanford, CA: Stanford University Press.

Cameron, Deborah. 1995. *Verbal Hygiene*. New York: Routledge.

Cook-Gumperz, Jenny. 1986. *The Social Construction of Literacy*. New York: Cambridge University Press.

Cooper, Marilyn. 1989. "Why Are We Talking About Discourse Communities? Or, Foundationalism Rears Its Ugly Head Once More." In *Writing as Social Action*, by Marilyn M. Cooper and Michael Holzman, 202–20. Portsmouth, NH: Boynton/Cook.

———. 1994. "Really Useful Knowledge: A Cultural Studies Agenda for Writing Centers." *The Writing Center Journal* 14 (2): 97–111.

Cornelius, Janet Duitsman. 1992. *When I Can Read My Title Clear: Literacy, Slavery, and Religion in the Antebellum South*. Columbia, SC: University of South Carolina Press.

Delpit, Lisa. 1988. "The Silenced Dialogue: Power and Pedagogy in Educating Other People's Children." *Harvard Educational Review* 58 (3): 280–98.

———. 1995. *Other People's Children: Cultural Conflict in the Classroom*. New York: The New Press.

DiPardo, Anne. 1992. "'Whispers of Coming and Going': Lessons from Fannie." *The Writing Center Journal* 12 (2): 125–44.

———. 1993. *A Kind of Passport: A Basic Writing Adjunct Program and the Challenge of Student Diversity*. Urbana, IL: National Council of Teachers of English.

Donald, James. 1993. "Literacy and the Limits of Democracy." In *The Insistence of the Letter*, edited by Bill Green, 120–36. Pittsburgh, PA: University of Pittsburgh Press.

Duster, Troy. 1995. "They're Taking Over! and Other Myths About Race on Campus." In *Higher Education Under Fire: Politics, Economics, and the Crisis of the Humanities*, edited by Michael Berube and Cary Nelson, 276–83. New York: Routledge.

Eagleton, Terry. 1991. *Ideology*. New York: Verso.

Ehrenreich, Barbara. 1989. *Fear of Falling: The Inner Life of the Middle Class*. New York: Pantheon.

Ellsworth, Elizabeth. 1989. "Why Doesn't This Feel Empowering? Working Through the Repressive Myths of Critical Pedagogy." *Harvard Educational Review* 59 (3): 297–324.

Erickson, Frederick. 1988. "School Literacy, Reasoning, and Civility: An Anthropologist's Perspective." In *Perspectives on Literacy*, edited by Eugene R.

Kintgen, Barry M. Kroll, and Mike Rose, 205–26. Carbondale, IL: Southern Illinois University Press.

Faigley, Lester. 1992. *Fragments of Rationality: Postmodernity and the Subject of Composition.* Pittsburgh, PA: University of Pittsburgh Press.

Fiumara, Gemma Corradi. 1990. *The Other Side of Language: A Philosophy of Listening.* London: Routledge.

Flax, Jane. 1993. *Disputed Subjects: Essays on Psychoanalysis, Politics, and Philosophy.* New York: Routledge.

Foucault, Michel. 1972. *The Archaeology of Knowledge and The Discourse on Language,* translated by A. M. Sheridan Smith. New York: Pantheon.

———. 1979. *Discipline and Punish: The Birth of the Prison.* New York: Vintage Books.

———. 1982. "The Subject and Power." In *Michel Foucault: Beyond Structuralism and Hermeneutics,* edited by Hubert L. Dreyfus and Paul Rabinow. Chicago: University of Chicago Press.

Fountaine, Tim. 1993. "'The Writing Center at My House': Listening to the Voices of Home Literacy." Annual Conference on College Composition and Communication, San Diego, CA.

Fox, Helen. 1994. *Listening to the World: Cultural Issues in Academic Writing.* Urbana, IL: National Council of Teachers of English.

Freire, Paulo. 1973. *Education for Critical Consciousness.* New York: The Seabury Press.

Gage, John T. 1987. *The Shape of Reason: Argumentative Writing in College.* New York: Macmillan.

Gardner, Howard. 1991. *The Unschooled Mind: How Children Think and How Schools Should Teach.* New York: Basic Books.

Gee, James Paul. 1996. *Social Linguistics and Literacies: Ideology in Discourses.* 2d ed. London: Taylor & Francis.

Gergen, Kenneth. 1991. *The Saturated Self: Dilemmas of Identity in Contemporary Life.* New York: Basic Books.

Gillam, Alice. 1994. "Collaborative Learning Theory and Peer Tutoring Practice." In *Intersections: Theory-Practice in the Writing Center,* edited by Joan A. Mullin and Ray Wallace, 39–53. Urbana, IL: National Council of Teachers of English.

Graff, Harvey J. 1991a. *The Legacies of Literacy: Continuities and Contradictions in Western Culture and Society.* Bloomington, IN: Indiana University Press.

———. 1991b. *The Literacy Myth: Cultural Integration and Social Structure in the Nineteenth Century.* New Brunswick, NJ: Transaction.

Gramsci, Antonio. 1971. *Selections from the Prison Notebooks,* edited and translated by Quintin Hoare and Geoffrey Nowell Smith. New York: International.

Grimm, Nancy, and Marsha Penti with Jeff Barrett, Rebecca Townsend, and Suhail Islam. 1998. "Rethinking Agency." In *Weaving Knowledge Together:*

Writing Centers and Collaboration, edited by Carol Peterson Haviland, Maria Notarangelo, Lene Whitley-Putz, and Thia Wolf, 194–217. Emmitsburg, MD: NWCA Press.

Grumet, Madeleine R. 1988. *Bitter Milk: Women and Teaching.* Amherst, MA: University of Massachusetts Press.

Hall, Stuart. 1986. "On Postmodernism and Articulation." *Journal of Communication Inquiry* 10: 45–60.

Harris, Joseph. 1989. "The Idea of Community in the Study of Writing." *College Composition and Communication* 40 (February): 11–22.

———. 1997. *A Teaching Subject: Composition Since 1966.* Upper Saddle River, NJ: Prentice Hall.

Harris, Muriel. 1995. "Talking in the Middle: Why Writers Need Writing Tutors." *College English* 57: 27–42.

Heath, Shirley Brice. 1983. *Ways with Words: Language, Life, and Work in Communities and Classrooms.* Cambridge: Cambridge University Press.

———. 1988. "Protean Shapes in Literacy Events: Ever-Shifting Oral and Literate Traditions." In *Perspectives on Literacy,* edited by Eugene R. Kintgen, Barry M. Kroll, and Mike Rose. Carbondale, IL: Southern Illinois University Press.

Heath, Shirley Brice, and Leslie Mangiola. 1991. *Children of Promise: Literate Activity in Linguistically and Culturally Diverse Classrooms.* Washington, DC: National Education Association.

Helmers, Marguerite H. 1994. *Writing Students: Composition Testimonials and Representations of Students.* Albany, NY: SUNY Press.

Herzberg, Bruce. 1994. "Community Service and Critical Teaching." *College Composition and Communication* 43 (3): 307–19.

hooks, bell. 1990. *Yearning: Race, Gender, and Cultural Politics.* Boston: South End Press.

———. 1993. *Sisters of the Yam: Black Women and Self-Recovery.* Boston: South End Press.

Hull, Glynda, and Mike Rose. 1990. "'This Wooden Shack Place': The Logic of an Unconventional Reading." *College Composition and Communication* 41 (3): 287–98.

Hull, Glynda, Mike Rose, Kay Losey Fraser, and Marisa Castellano. 1991. "Remediation as a Social Construct: Perspectives from an Analysis of Classroom Discourse." *College Composition and Communication* 42 (3): 299–329.

Jameson, Fredric. 1992. *Postmodernism or the Cultural Logic of Late Capitalism.* Durham, NC: Duke University Press.

Johnson, Richard. 1986/87. "What Is Cultural Studies Anyway?" *Social Text* 16 (Winter): 38–80.

Kinkead, Joyce A., and Jeanette G. Harris, eds. 1993. *Writing Centers in Context: Twelve Case Studies.* Urbana, IL: National Council of Teachers of English.

Kitalong-Will, Ann. 1998. "Practicing Ideology: Examining Pronominal Choice in Writing Center Practice." Unpublished paper.

Kress, Gunther. 1997. *Before Writing: Rethinking the Paths to Literacy.* London: Routledge.

Laclau, Ernesto, and Chantal Mouffe. 1985. *Hegemony & Socialist Strategy.* London: Verso.

Lather, Patti. 1991. *Getting Smart: Feminist Research and Pedagogy with/in the Postmodern.* New York: Routledge.

Lerner, Harriet Goldhor. 1985. *The Dance of Anger: A Woman's Guide to Changing the Patterns of Intimate Relationships.* New York: Harper & Row.

———. 1989. *The Dance of Intimacy: A Woman's Guide to Courageous Acts of Change in Key Relationships.* New York: Harper & Row.

———. 1993. *The Dance of Deception: Pretending and Truth-Telling in Women's Lives.* New York: HarperCollins.

Loewen, James W. 1995. *Lies My Teacher Told Me: Everything Your American History Textbook Got Wrong.* New York: The New Press.

Lotto, Edward. "The Angel of the House: Writing Centers and Departments of English." Unpublished manuscript.

Lu, Min-Zhan. 1994. "Professing Multiculturalism: The Politics of Style in the Contact Zone." *College Composition and Communication* 45 (4): 442–58.

Matthews, Sylvia, and Hajj Flemings. 1995. "Seeing from the Inside Out and the Outside In." National Writing Centers Association Conference, St. Louis, Missouri, September.

McDonald, Robert L. 1994. "An Interview with James Berlin." *Composition Studies* 22 (1): 25–43.

Miller, Susan. 1991. *Textual Carnivals: The Politics of Composition.* Carbondale, IL: Southern Illinois University Press.

Mouffe, Chantal. 1992. "Feminism, Citizenship, and Radical Democratic Politics." In *Feminists Theorize the Political,* edited by Judith Butler and Joan W. Scott, 369–84. New York: Routledge.

Myers, Miles. 1996. *Changing Our Minds: Negotiating English and Literacy.* Urbana, IL: National Council of Teachers of English.

New London Group. 1996. "A Pedagogy of Multiliteracies: Designing Social Futures." *Harvard Educational Review* 66: 60–92.

North, Stephen M. 1984a. "The Idea of a Writing Center." *College English* 46 (5): 433–46.

———. 1984b. "Writing Center Research: Testing Our Assumptions." In *Writing Centers: Theory and Administration,* edited by Gary A. Olson, 24–35. Urbana, IL: National Council of Teachers of English.

Ogbu, John U. 1987. "Opportunity Structure, Cultural Boundaries, and Literacy." In *Language, Literacy, and Culture: Issues of Society and Schooling,* edited by Judith A. Langer. Norwood, NJ: Ablex.

Ohmann, Richard. 1988. *Politics of Letters.* Middletown, CT: Wesleyan University Press.

Olson, Gary A., and Evelyn Ashton-Jones. 1988. "Writing Center Directors: The Search for Professional Status." *WPA: Writing Program Administration* 12 (1–2): 19–28.

Pearson, Carol, Donna Shavlik, and Judith Touchton, eds. 1989. *Educating the Majority.* New York: Macmillan.

Penti, Marsha Elizabeth. 1992. "Writing Centers as Spaces for Negotiating Difference." Midwest Writing Centers Association, St. Paul, MN.

———. 1998. "Religious Identities in Student Writing: Understanding Students of Difference." Ph.D. diss., Michigan Technological University.

Pratt, Mary Louise. 1991."Arts of the Contact Zone." *Profession* 91: 33–40.

Raymond, James C. 1989. "Rhetoric as Bricolage: Theory and Its Limits in Legal and Other Sorts of Discourse." In *Worlds of Writing: Teaching and Learning in Discourse Communities of Work,* edited by Carolyn Matalene, 388–97. New York: Random House.

Resnick, Daniel, and Lauren B. Resnick. 1977. "The Nature of Literacy: An Historical Exploration." *Harvard Educational Review* 47: 370–85.

Rose, Mike. 1989. *Lives on the Boundary: The Struggles and Achievements of America's Underprepared.* New York: Free Press.

Roy, Alice. 1995. "The Grammar and Rhetoric of Inclusion." *College English* 57 (2): 182–95.

Schutz, Aaron, and Anne Ruggles Gere. 1998. "Service Learning and English Studies." *College English* 60 (2): 129–49.

Scribner, Sylvia, and Michael Cole. 1988. "Unpackaging Literacy." In *Perspectives on Literacy,* edited by Eugene R. Kintgen, Barry M. Kroll, and Mike Rose, 57–70. Carbondale, IL: Southern Illinois University Press.

Severino, Carol. 1992. "Where the Cultures of Basic Writers and Academia Intersect: Cultivating the Common Ground." *Journal of Basic Writing* 11 (1): 4–15.

Smith, Louise Z. 1991. "Family Systems Theory and the Form of Conference Dialogue." *The Writing Center Journal* 11 (2): 61–72.

Spooner, Michael. 1993. "Circles and Centers: Some Thoughts on the Writing Center and Academic Book Publishing." *Writing Lab Newsletter* 17 (10): 1–3.

Steinem, Gloria. 1992. *Revolution from Within: A Book of Self-Esteem.* Boston: Little, Brown.

Street, Brian V. 1984. *Literacy in Theory and Practice.* Cambridge: Cambridge University Press.

———. 1995. *Social Literacies: Critical Approaches to Literacy in Development, Ethnography and Education.* London: Longman.

Trachsel, Mary. 1995. "Nurturant Ethics and Academic Ideals: Convergence in the Writing Center." *The Writing Center Journal* 16 (1): 24–45.

Trimbur, John. 1991. "Literacy and the Discourse of Crisis." In *The Politics of Writing Instruction: Postsecondary,* edited by Richard Bullock, John Trimbur, and Chuck Schuster, 277–95. Portsmouth, NH: Boynton/Cook.

Tzu, Sun. 1993. *The Art of War,* translated by Thomas Cleary. Boston: Shambhala.

Villanueva, Jr., Victor. 1993. *Bootstraps: From an American Academic of Color.* Urbana, IL: National Council of Teachers of English.

Vygotsky, Lev. 1988. *Thought and Language.* Cambridge, MA: The MIT Press.

Welch, Nancy. 1997. *Getting Restless: Rethinking Revision in Writing Instruction.* Portsmouth, NH: Boynton/Cook.

Williams, Patricia J. 1997. *Seeing a Color-Blind Future: The Paradox of Race.* New York: Noonday Press.

Williams, Raymond. 1976. *Keywords: A Vocabulary of Culture and Society.* New York: Oxford University Press.

———. 1977. *Marxism and Literature.* New York: Oxford University Press.

Wood, Denis. 1992. *The Power of Maps.* New York: Guilford Press.

Young, Iris Marion. 1990. *Justice and the Politics of Difference.* Princeton, NJ: Princeton University Press.

———. 1997. *Intersecting Voices: Dilemmas of Gender, Political Philosophy, and Policy.* Princeton, NJ: Princeton University Press.

Index